The Work of Ettore Sottsass and Associates

The Work of Ettore Sottsass and Associates

Edited by Milco Carboni

Written by Andrea Branzi, Herbert Muschamp,
Gianni Pettena, Barbara Radice, Patrizia Ranzo

Universe

This book was produced in association with Sottsass
Associates.

Special thanks to Barbara Radice, Helmut Newton, Santi
Caleca, Bruno Bischofberger Gallery, Gallery Mourmans

First published in the United States of America in 1999
by UNIVERSE PUBLISHING
A Division of Rizzoli International Publications, Inc.
300 Park Avenue South
New York, NY 10010

99 00 01 02 / 10 9 8 7 6 5 4 3 2 1

Library of Congress Cataloging-in-Publication Data:
The Work of Ettore Sottsass and Associates / edited by Milco
Carboni ; written by Andrea Branzi . . . [et al.].
    p.   cm.
    Published in association with an exhibition that originates
in Milan.
    Includes bibliographical references.
    ISBN 0-7893-0358-2
    1. Sottsass, Ettore, 1917–   Exhibitions. 2. Sottsass
associati (Milan, Italy) Exhibitions. I. Carboni, Milco. II.
Branzi, Andrea.
NA 1123.S66A4 1999
720'.92—dc21   99-24964 CIP

Frontispiece: Detail of the stairs of the Esprit shop in Cologne
page 8: Wolf House in Colorado
page 9: Sketch by Ettore Sottsass of the section of Wolf
House.

Design by Sottsass Associates/
Paola Lambardi, Mario Milizia

Printed in Italy

Contents

Sottsass Associates from 1980 to today
Daniel Aeschbacher, Anna Allegro, Flávia Alves de Souza, Michael
Armani, Fabio Azzolina, Federica Barbiero, Michele Barro, Veronica
Bass, Martine Bedin, Dante Bega, Elide Bega, Johnny Benson,
Alberto Berengo Gardin, Cora Bishofberger, Pietro Bongiana,
Manuela Boniforti, Guido Borelli, Ambrogio Borsani, Viviana Bottero,
Laurent Bourgois, Edoardo Brambilla, Ulrike Broeking, Ruth Cabella,
El Cannibal, Milco Carboni, Beppe Caturegli, Liana Cavallaro, Franco
Cervi, Aldo Cibic, Annalisa Citterio, Elena Cutolo, Alberto Davila,
Elisabetta Della Torre, Monica Del Torchio, Giuseppe Del Greco,
Claudio Dell'Olio, Paolo De Lucchi, José de Rivera Marinello, Cristina
Di Carlo, Simone Dreyfuss, Richard Eisermann, Bonni Evensen,
Blanca Ferrer, Peter Flint, Franca Foianini, Eugenia Folci, Maya Fong,
Giovanella Formica, Barbara Forni, Riccardo Forti, Maria Paola Frau,
Raffaella Galli, Massimo Giacon, Susanna Giancolombo, Paola
Giovinelli, Annette Glatzel, Bruna Gnocchi, Theo Gonser, Nuala
Goodman, Johanna Grawunder, Valentina Grego, Gertrud Gruber,
Valentina Hermann, Shuji Hisada, Hugh Huddleson, James Irvine,
Fumiko Itoh, Takeaki Kaneko, Maki Kasano, Paola Lambardi, Annette
Lang, Larry Lasky, Oliver Layseca, Tina Leimbacher, Catharina
Lorenz, Franco Luchini, Mercedes Jaén Ruiz, Nathalie Jean, Mona
Kim, Walter Kirpisenko, Christopher Kirwan, Francia Knapp Mooney,
Ron Kopels, Donato Maino, Marco Marabelli, Loredana Martinelli,
Frédéric Mas, Cristina Massocchi, Luciana Mastropasqua, Cecilia
Mazzone, Lorenzo Meccoli, Patrick Mellet, Costanza Melli, Sergio
Menichelli, Monica Merlo, Mario Milizia, Yasukio Miwa, Alba Monti,
Sebastiano Mosterts, Gianluigi Mutti, Davide Nardi, Nicola Nicolaidis,
Jon Otis, Caterina Padova, Massimo Penati, Laura Persico, Massimo
Pertosa, ,Susan Phelps, Adalberto Pironi, Roberto Pollastri, Marco
Polloni, Timothy Power, Antonella Provasi, Christoph Radl, Elisabetta
Redaelli, Christopher Redfern, Maria Marta Rey Rosa, Douglas
Riccardi, Sara Ricciardi, Nicoletta Roia, Francisco Romero, Riccarda
Ruberl, Mike Ryan, Giusi Salvadè, Maria Sanchez, Paolo Sancis, John
Sandell, Mika Sato, Sabina Scornavacca, George Scott, David Shaw
Nicholls, Eugenia Sicolo, Tony Smart, Ettore Sottsass, Vittorio
Spaggiari, Antonella Spiezio, Jenny Stein, Marco Susani, Ken Suzuki,
Gerard Taylor, Giacomo Tedeschi, Flavia Thumshirn, Matteo Thun,
Viviana Trapani, Jorge Vadillo, Susan Verba, Tiziano Vudafieri, Anna
Wagner, Wendy Wheatley, Gail Wittwer, Bill Wurz, Yasuo Yamawaki,
Carla Zanelli, Marco Zanini, Neven Zoricic.

Projects

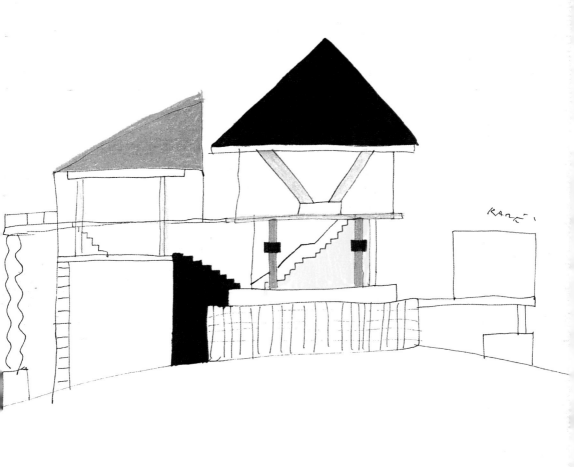

Ettore Sottsass. <u>Untitled</u>. India ink on paper, 1992.

Formal Quality in the World

Andrea Branzi

The contribution that I can make to the work of Ettore Sottsass is to attempt to place his professional career, and the history of our friendship, within a larger picture—within postwar as well as contemporary design history.

The curious thing about Ettore is that he appears to be an architect totally immersed in his own formal logic, his drawings, and thoughts. He is, therefore, an artist and intellectual fully represented in his private output, with no waste or imperfections. From a different angle, though, we find that he has always been at the hub of very broad cultural movements that have transformed our discipline in the past forty years.

Ettore seems like an ascetic at the center of an everlasting fray provoked by him personally—through not words, but deeds. He is a cantankerous character who has cultivated a number of deep and lasting friendships.

Barbara Radice writes that Ettore doesn't even know what friendship is. Indeed, the very few friendships that he has cultivated are based not on plain liking or trust, but on a shared cultural militancy. They rest on joint participation in a tough battle of ideas—the only one that matters in life.

For Ettore, like very few, is a militant architect. He is a professional practitioner of his own ideas rather than of his designs. Our friendship, too, is based on this militancy and on its consequent solidarity and affection.

The architect's craft is commonly perceived as a means and not as an end. Our battles, if one looks at them closely, are never about design, but more about man's destiny and its relation to the vicissitudes of industrialism.

I shall try, therefore, to identify the fundamental insights of his work—the structures of his thinking and the great intuitiveness that ultimately make his work different from that of other leading designers of his time—in order to understand the vast influence he has wielded in postwar design.

Ettore's background and context are those of Italian design as we mean it—as an experimental workshop on an international scale. In other words, as a practical field in which decisions are made that not only have an Italian specificity, but also a broader scale that embraces history and the major issues of our industrial system.

This is not a generically internationalist, or worse, colonialist attitude. It is rather a sort of historical defect, corresponding to an attitude typical of very old countries that have had great responsibilities and suffered great decadence. This attitude—this sense of vast responsibility—is common to all of Europe, but in Ettore it is doubly present on account of his Italian and Austrian origins. What tires him is not his work, but the responsibility that the work ultimately requires in the face of human tragedies and joys, which are always intermingled.

The apparent joy of Ettore's signs stems from the intrinsically dramatic quality of all his work. The playful smile is tinged with a consciousness of man's solitude and a commitment to offering him implements and flowers for his solitary existence.

The context of postwar Italian design in which the young Sottsass—having survived the war and imprisonment at Sarajevo—started to work was one of physical and political destruction whose past had been removed and whose future was faced without any methodology.

The postwar cultural climate in Italy was characterized by a will to design against something, because that was also the only way of designing in favor of something. People were not looking, as they were in Germany, for scientific certainties in design. On the contrary, they found it exciting to open up new possibilities. The idea of an imperfect, problematic, and expanding modernity had already taken shape; it was already a somewhat postindustrial idea because it was based on systems of weakness and separation.

The Italian designer's dealings were with industry. Both sides, however, retained and defended their autonomy, holding it up as a mutual asset. The designer did not feel he

was just a technician, and industry minded its own business instead of embarking on cultural crusades. Arranged in this way, the marriage worked well.

In Italy designers and industrialists were actually both part of the opposition, since they tried to encourage processes of modernization, which central governments prevented by defending the interests of the middle classes against industrial capital and against reformist intellectuals.

The postwar atmosphere in Italy, therefore, was a controversial, provincial one bursting with talent, inspired by the urge to create a state of discontinuity rather than large-scale social and environmental continuities. In Italy—unlike other nations in which an absolutist vision of industrial modernization was being promoted—designers worked with the greatest of ease as much for mass production as for the local Brianza carpenter. It was a country in which new standard languages and also anarchic and heretical signs were being sought; where high technologies were being approached, but also wood-pith or wrought iron. It was a country that believed in progress, but also in the art of mediation and in the idea of progress based on intuition as well as science.

So it was in a fertile, richly original and creative environment that the young Sottsass found himself during the postwar period in Italy. In it, however, there existed the taboo of increased consumer spending. The cream of European design had already firmly adopted the logic of industrial production since the Bauhaus days. It looked upon consumer

Ettore Sottsass. <u>Ring</u>. 1963.

goods as a dangerous deformation of modernity—an attack on the rationality of civilized and technological development.

Tomás Maldonado's school at Ulm dominated the design debate in the '50s with an idea of Europe as seen through the eyes of an Argentinean. With Calvinistic morality he devised a scientific theory of design based entirely on an analysis of technologies and constructive processes, but directed toward the freezing and forestalling of any emotive involvement by the consumer, thus suppressing the generating of goods even by their form. The product had to be a rational reality for a highly industrialized rational society.

What this boiled down to was an entirely unmanageable contradiction, geared to an impracticable idea of development of order and entailing the repression of exceptions and the leveling of complexity, which are instead the specific characteristics of capitalism, of the free market, and of the development of industrialism itself.

The hegemonic parties of those years in Italy, the Catholics, and the Communists, were for different reasons against any increase in consumption and in favor of the protection of traditional education.

Thus, in Italy between the economic boom and the early '60s, the debate stiffened, and design pursued a dangerous involution, collaborating on a political (programmed economy) and cultural (programmed art) model in the manner of a terza via—without any real prospects and with its development blocked.

In this moralistic and provincial context, Ettore assumed an absolutely independent and original approach that in time was to assert a great influence, making him a point of reference for diverse cultural hypotheses that were to mature later on, thanks also to the contribution of a new generation of designers.

Unlike the Italian architects of his age group, he followed a different formative path, aiming right away for a broad international scale.

In 1961 he made two very long journeys that were to completely shift the DNA of his cultural makeup.

The first pivotal journey was to India (with Ceylon, Nepal, and Burma). It was not the usual journey into architecture; what Ettore derived from it was not a linguistic or formal resource, but the basis for an existential philosophy that was to accompany him always.

This philosophy, acquired in the immense hot and exciting belly of India, amounted to a global acceptance, as it were, of the cosmos, of its laws and tragedies, and of history. It was an acceptance not without criticism, not indifferent, but based on the shifting of critical and selective systems—typical of our Catholic and rationalist culture—toward a planetary consciousness, a simultaneous vision of good and evil and of life and death. All this is typical of oriental culture and of India—it produces a tragic outward and inner calm, and a heroic energy that no longer fears anything.

In that same year, he traveled to America to be treated in Palo Alto for a grave form of

Ettore Sottsass, <u>Efira</u>, vase in blown glass, Memphis, 1986.

Ettore Sottsass, <u>Lemon Sherbet</u>, furniture in wood, Plexiglas, and glass mosaic, Blum Helman, 1987.

nephrosis that took him to the brink of death. When he recovered, and began to mix closely with the colony of West Coast Beat poets (Allen Ginsberg, Jack Kerouac, Gregory Corso, Lawrence Ferlinghetti, Bob Dylan, etc.), whose works his wife Nanda was translating into Italian, Ettore's mind-set was already totally predisposed to understanding the budding new civilization.

From his hospital room Ettore sent out a sort of newsletter to his friends. It was titled "East 128," after the wing of the hospital where he was staying. The graphic design was already totally outside the tradition of rationalist layouts that were all the rage in Europe; it was also beyond the emerging American pop art and its absolute realism. "East 128" was a philosophical statement based on the stratification of commercial images, pages that were a segment of an infinite and dense fabric of communications, signs, and information—in short, a sandwich of all things existent. There was no trace of elegance in it, but none of vulgarity either. It presented an immersion in and overall acceptance of a cosmology before which old instruments of judgment and preconceived rejection had become meaningless.

This taking possession of reality—this profound, preliminary immersion in the existent—was similar to a Nietzschean concept of the acceptance of history. Its origins lay in India as Ettore has always understood it—as existing outside of morality and politics, and before architecture.

His adhesion to consumer culture, as a superseding of the old European rationalism,

was therefore very particular. He was never a pop artist like the Americans, nor a true radical designer like the young Italians. Ettore accepted America through India—indeed, they were two ways of looking at the same problem. Poverty and abundance are but two sides of the same coin, or two characters in the same story. In fact, when he returned to Italy in 1967 he exhibited at the Sperone Gallery in Milan a group of large ceramics that he significantly titled "Menhir, Ziggurat, Stupas, Hydrants and Gas Pumps"—that is, religious objects and consumer objects.

Everything is part of a great life cycle; this is the lesson Ettore also learned from his friends the Beat poets of the West Coast. For them Zen went hand in hand with canned food and nomadism with mass high technologies, in a liberated vision of existence.

From the Beat poets he learned—and this is very important—to appreciate a different dimension of the concept of politics. It no longer coincided with major ideological and social programs, but with the practice of a creativity linked to life. Literature and existence, as Barbara Radice notes, were for them the same thing, which meant that for Ettore aesthetics became a political value. His background, so different from that of late-rationalist European designers or of those who were engaged as intellectuals, found at once a great affinity with the emerging Italian avant-garde groups, and particularly with the ones he met in Florence in 1966.

We too, like our entire generation, were influenced by Beat philosophy. We too were a militant part of pop art, but our background was totally different, and our mischief, too, was a long way from the Hindu pacifism with which Ettore presented himself, almost as a flower child, wearing his hair long and bells on his feet.

Although he went through the period of radical architecture as a protagonist, Ettore was never a truly radical designer. That revolutionary period did not shift by one millimeter his way of operating—on the contrary, it confirmed it. In the explosive climate of the young avant-garde groups in Florence, Ettore found the right atmospheric pressure—a context deeply committed to the renewal of the culture of design in its modes, signs, and concepts. He found important intellectual relationships, and also fellow-travelers who were courageous, although different from him. Most importantly, he brought with him—in the radical period between 1966 and 1972—his mature anthropological side, and an already established professional presence.

In this sense his role—precisely because it was indirect—was absolutely fundamental to the quality, growth, and above all to the continuity of the Italian movement.

In Britain, France, and Austria, the radical period—once its revolutionary acme had passed—left a number of prominent new figures on the scene (Peter Cook, Hans Hollein, Coop Himmelblau), and a general ebb into uncertainty. In Italy, on the other hand, during the 1970s and 1980s Nuovo Design grew culturally and professionally to become the principal movement of post-industrial culture, in a continuous unfold-

ing of relationships, initiatives (Alchymia and Memphis), new issues, and topics of investigation.

All of us younger people were engaged in polemical processes. To embrace consumer culture, as it had been both promoted and contested by pop art, by the Beat Generation, by English rock music, and by new fashion, was a way of developing a different, global modernization—not only in the forms of urban and domestic landscapes, but also in public and private behavior.

It was a way of heightening the integration but also the contradictions of the system. The whole of the 1968 generation that we belonged to was moving within these contradictions with exasperating confidence—at that time the idea that uncertainty might be the really great political novelty and that experimentalism might be a new operational category was absolutely nonexistent.

All this was to be a conquest accomplished with difficulty in the decades that followed; but then, in the Europe of 1968, politics still meant a search for and an affirmation of systems of truth, and this affirmation took place in a spoken (or shouted) form and through street demonstrations.

Ettore had no kind of relationship at all with all this. Indeed, he had and still has no kind of relationship with politics as a system of indisputable certainties, as verbal activity, and in any case as a practice incapable of producing positive effects on man's everyday and cosmic existence.

Ettore remained deeply confident in his system of uncertainties and in the idea that

Ettore Sottsass. <u>Untitled</u>. India ink on paper, 1992.

the renewal of society was a cultural, not a political matter. He therefore viewed with some concern the harsh requisition of all the places in existence by a declamatory and violent political activity. He saw a threat to that extraordinary creative and fertile heritage, which the pre-1968 generation had built up with great courage, in daily life and in culture.

In some ways the real victim of 1968 was in fact the pre-1968 generation and not the middle class. The latter lost nothing, because it played a leading role in the psychodrama performed entirely within its womb. The principal actors of the pre-1968 period, on the other hand, saw their worktables and their pacifist hopes overturned. They were confronted by fascist thugs (Ettore was beaten up in Milan's Galleria because of his long hair and his Indian chieftain's headgear) as well as by workers on factory committees, who at Poltronova played "The Red Flag" from their indoor loudspeakers and demanded that management stop making Ettore's useless furniture.

Ettore had arrived at the period of radical architecture not only already a radical, by virtue of his long-standing links with the movement and with the philosophy of a new civilization, but also with a professional maturity that was entirely absent in the generation of his young fellow-adventurers.

For Olivetti, Ettore had already designed the first large electronic computer, the Elea 9003, in 1959, and the Tecne 3 typewriter, in 1964.

Here I would like, however, to talk about his work for big industry from a different point of view. Because the history of Ettore's relationship with Olivetti needs to be analyzed not only for its results, but for the inspired and absolutely original formula on which it was based. It was one of Ettore's most important and fundamental intuitions, described as follows by Barbara Radice:

"Ettore began working at Olivetti as a freelancer until, in the early '60s, Roberto offered him a full-time job at Olivetti on a very high salary. After thinking it over at length, Ettore refused and, typically, counterproposed to Roberto an absolutely new system of dealings between the corporation and the designers, which he accepted. It worked very well then and is still working well thirty years later.

"Ettore asked the corporation to open a design studio with collaborators paid by Olivetti and with an administration led by Olivetti, but chosen by him. He would remain a freelance collaborator and would direct the studio, whose chief designers were to maintain a freelance relationship with the company.

"The solution was a brilliant one because it settled various problems to everybody's advantage and satisfaction. On one hand the designers, with the freedom to work for themselves, were not swallowed up and more or less destroyed and dried up by the routine and by the internal struggles of an industrial environment, and on the other their freelance contract with the outside ensured the exchange of ideas and a greater possibility of being culturally up-to-date.

"The studio was opened and from the

Ettore Sottsass, <u>Untitled</u>, watercolor on paper, 1989.

beginning Ettore sought international collaborators such as Hans Von Klier, Andries Van Onk, George Sowden, Masanori Umeda, and Tiger Tateishi. In the 1960s and '70s the Olivetti office at via Manzoni 14 in Milan was one of the most interesting and innovative international design centers. Thanks to his friendship with Roberto and to his freelance position, Ettore enjoyed a specially privileged relationship with Olivetti. He was responsible to Roberto and no one else, and with him, marketing management, engineering designers, and production management, he sat at the decision-making table where programs that concerned the company's general image and industry strategy were discussed and deliberated."

Therefore, while those who were considered to be the leading front for design theory were devising a model in Germany for the integration of designers into big industry, a different model was emerging in Italy, which was to prove in every way a winner, based on the idea of reciprocal autonomy. In this model,

design was not an industrial function used only to resolve production problems, but a strategic activity and a civilized culture immersed in the changing of history and therefore able to give big industry, through design, an identity within society. Ettore's was the prophetic vision of an open industry that does not intend to integrate society and culture, but instead to find its place within these spheres so as to offer new opportunities for development—a vision that also matched the Waldensian morality of Adriano Olivetti, who was committed to the reformist movement "Comunità."

This singularly original vision bore great fruits not only at Olivetti, but throughout the Italian design system which has always used that formula as a reference. Today it is once again of great topical interest, at a time when all Western (but also Eastern) industry is striving to overcome a serious economic and geopolitical crisis, and is creating a new system for developing and establishing new strategic connections with design.

Opposite page: Ettore Sottsass, Coming Back from Spain, Long Ago, furniture unit in wood, Plexiglas, and steel, Blum Helman, 1987.

From Radicals to Memphis

Gianni Pettena

Experimentation and innovation within the discipline were already evident in the 1950s in designs put forth by the Japanese "Metabolists"—mostly students and assistants of Kenzo Tange, such as Arata Isozaki, and Kyonori Kikutake—and by others, known as "utopists." It was, however, the design concepts and insights of the London group Archigram that really launched a radical process of revising and creating a new foundation for architecture and for its chief means of communication: design. Archigram was made up of students and fellow travelers who had emerged from that splendid place— the school animated by Alvin Boyarsky—the Architectural Association in Bedford Square, London. It was a place where at the time, besides Peter Cook and the other members of Archigram, it was possible to run into all the people with whom we would eventually establish a long-distance dialogue through writings or designs that appeared in exhibitions or magazines, from Paris to Berlin, Turin, Milan, or Venice. We also communicated through small publications or through word of mouth, perhaps even unconsciously involved in the same course of investigation, though nearly always via solitary routes.

The course of innovation pursued by Archigram relied on the insertion of color and supergraphics, as well as countless ironic touches into a project for a hyper-technological city—a gigantic and robotic elephant for an unspecified future. Austrian investigations, on the other hand, were more closely attuned to experimentation in the visual arts. Hollein and Pichler's manifesto, Peintner's drawings, and the performances of Haus Rucker Co. or Salz der Erde, acquired the composite characteristics of conceptual and linguistic overlapping typical of a culture subject to aging and deterioration. From this awareness emerged liberating ideas that anticipated a provocative, refreshing design that departed from an inherited geometrical order and that was richly endowed with linguistic metaphors and innovations. The ideas ranged from performances to furniture, interiors, architecture, and brief theoretical texts, all of which revealed a close relationship to contemporaneous experimentation in the European and American visual arts.

In Italy the experiments of the second half of the 1960s (originating in Florence and Milan) expressed in the most articulate and complex way the emergence of a design concept that was perfectly in tune with the natural evolution of youth culture of the time and that served as an orthodox interpreter of that culture's maturation.

Ettore Sottsass, Furniture for Casa Tchou, 1960.

The exhibitions of British and American pop art (at the 1964 Venice Biennale), <u>arte povera</u>, and conceptual art were at that time clearly indispensable, inevitable references that affected every artistic pursuit. But there was—in the writings and visual displays that took the form of furniture, drawings, and ceramics by Sottsass—a way to anticipate the direction of every aspect of Italian experimentation during that period. The work that Sottsass did beginning in the early 1960s for Poltronova, Bitossi, and Abet Print, showed a surmounting of and a fresh nonchalance for limitations of scale, language, and conventions, and it pointed to possible itineraries of investigation with such naturalness and even facility that it was impossible not to feel the work's seductiveness.

The two original threads of what was later to be defined as the "radical" experiment—the Florentine Archizoom and Superstudio, and later Ufo and Pettena—were characterized in the first case by derivation and pop influences, and in the other by a relationship to <u>arte povera</u> and to conceptual and performance art. Neither, however, could be correctly understood if one did not also see in them the implicit consequence and influence of the work done by Sottsass at the time.

"Radical" experimentation in Italy had two characteristics largely influenced by Sottsass that distinguished it from the experimentation in Britain and Austria: furniture design and an abundance of theoretical writings.

The role and scale of furniture had entirely individual connotations for each of the "Florentine" experimenters, although they expressed a desire to become the synthesis of a true allegory of intentions, strategies, and ideologies. Archigram, Archizoom, Superstudio, and Hollein were all designing, therefore, and theorizing "global" interpretations, nonstop cities, aircraft-carrier cities, "continuous monuments." But only Archizoom, Superstudio, Ufo, and Pettena designed and produced allegorical and architectural furniture—furniture and interiors that were themselves manifestos but that preceded or followed real manifestos—theoretical texts or tools for comprehending and interpreting the complex system of "reality." This was precisely as Sottsass had done or was doing with his furniture for Poltronova or with his ceramics for Bitossi, which introduced us to a freedom previously unknown as far as material, color, and scale, and as he had done with texts published by Pianeta Fresco.

The early 1970s brought the possibility of a more regular exchange of experimental processes and concepts. These were hosted by La Pietra's magazine <u>In</u>, by exhibition catalogues such as those of the IDZ in Berlin directed by François Burkhardt, in Monica Pidgeon's <u>A.D.</u>, and above all by <u>Casabella</u>, which under the editorship of Alessandro Mendini ensured not only the continuity but also the richness and multiplicity of information, between the orthodox (projects by Gregotti) and the liberal (Germano Celant's land and conceptual art). Global Tools, the 1973 Milan Triennale, and later Alchymia were interconnected experiences that are fundamental to the understanding of the various phenomenologies that were to follow.

Text within the poster image:

"IL SESTANTE" VIA SPIGA 3

ETTORE SOTTSASS JR.

CERAMICHE DI SERIE

DAL 6 AL 16 DICEMBRE 1958

DISEGNATE PER IL "SESTANTE"

Ettore Sottsass, Poster for the exhibition Ceramiche di Serie (Mass-produced ceramics), Il Sestante Gallery, Milan, 1958.

With Global Tools a dream materialized—a place for exchange and comparison was set up among recognized fellow travelers. This also came to be called a school, whose founding teachers declared themselves, above all else, students themselves. The work of experimentation was specialized according to areas of "discipline" in which "common" experiences and design prototypes were concretized, while these activities were documented by university lectures, articles, and exhibitions. Here the different periods, other waves of different geographical locations, and successive "experimental" generations were brought together.

It was Andrea Branzi who gave this foundation its ideological and energetic thrust, generating critical investigations and well-organized results, such as participation by the radical sector in the 1973 Milan Triennale (with Sottsass as commissioner for the international design section and Branzi as coordinator). In those years, with Branzi's "Radical Notes" feature in Casabella, the writings of Mendini and Raggi, and the series of publications by Sottsass, Superstudio, Archizoom, Pettena, Ufo, and Dalisi, theory and experimentation mingled with what Celant, in particular, had brought from the visual arts to serve as a comparison (arte povera, conceptual art, and land art) within a shared platform of experimentation.

In 1977–78, with the furniture by Sottsass and Branzi for Croff Casa and later, in 1978–79, with Alchymia, are included the destinations, everyday objects, elements of interior design, and the first adaptations of forms for a viable industrial production. The furniture that had been produced in the preceding years tended to represent a "global" field of experimentation, to reintroduce concepts and to criticize and reconstruct strategies that "radically," and often ironically, revisited typologies and ideologies (the chair, sofa, totem, stupa, or ziggurat). With Alchymia, however, this analytical sequence of axiomatic definitions was suspended in favor of a design concept better able to interpret the typologies of daily life.

The work done by Sottsass seems to have moved in two main directions; in addition to the ceramics, the furniture for Poltronova, and the industrial design work for Olivetti, he devoted himself to a careful linguistic investigation—a conceptual reexamination whose experimentalism establishes a dialogue with contemporaneous experiences in the visual arts—that is expressed through laminate furniture, glass, ceramics, writings, and visionary drawings. We should mention the illustrations to the "Planet as Festival" for Casabella in 1972; the "Magic Carpet" for Bedding in 1974; the "Design Metaphors" of 1972–74; and outdoor installations, which Sottsass calls "constructions," and which a short while later would take shape in the ironic affirmations of his drawings (If I Were Rich, Very Rich, Eclectic Architecture, Who's Afraid of Frank Lloyd Wright), shown in the Presence/Absence exhibition of 1976.

Relationships with the Florentine groups were established in the early 1970s in Global Tools, and could be compared with other trends in exhibitions such as Italy: The New

Ettore Sottsass, Valentine portable typewriter, Olivetti, 1969.

Ettore Sottsass. Fiberglass furniture. Poltronova. 1970.

Domestic Landscape (New York, 1972), the 1973 Milan Triennale, the IDZ in Berlin, and Presence/Absence in Bologna, and continued to evolve and diversify through the 1970s, up to Alchymia in 1978–79. In the meantime these original fellow travelers were joined by a second wave of younger colleagues. Michele De Lucchi collaborated, independently, with Sottsass Associates; Marco Zanini, Marco Marabelli, Matteo Thun, and Aldo Cibic founded Sottsass Associates in 1980, subsequently welcoming Johanna Grawunder and Mike Ryan, Mario Milizia, and James Irvine.

As far as Sottsass Associates is concerned, there is not much difference between architecture and design—they are two aspects of the same creative process. Design is often an exercise in architecture. The process of inventing a design piece, on any scale, becomes an "opportunity" for architecture, an exercise in composition, or decomposition and re-aggregation. It follows that even small changes on the linguistic level—alphabet, grammar, and syntax—in a design process that is concerned with a simple everyday object or piece of furniture or interior belong to a broader design. They belong to an architecture designed around people's lives that has a disarming simplicity but that involves significant gestures, and a solemn ritual and complexity. They do not, however, go so far as to lose their sense of hierarchy and scale, sequence and surprise— elements perceived in silence and meditation. Every beginning and every intermediary passage, every concept articulated or developed and expressed through a language

or through the visual symbolism of a drawing, is an exercise in architecture.

Metaphors of architecture and design—the Memphis experience (the first show was held in 1981) also went through this process, identifying integrated relationships between objects, the environment, and architecture. These elements of different complexities in a unique process of spatial invention tended toward the best and most balanced structural and linguistic intensity. Memphis assimilated the process of critical analysis conducted in the "radical" period (ending with the last major Alchymia exhibitions at the end of the 1970s). It seemed to be saying what nobody wanted to hear, what everyone was by then ready to hear, in that way and with such intensity. Many felt it was the only possible response to conformity and anonymity and to the obtuseness of so many—rationalist or other—translations and reexaminations.

For Sottsass Associates, however, this meant an urge to accelerate and to push themselves toward more complex ideas. This new maturity of language and new conceptual structures of interpretation subsequently led them to an approach that would lean more and more in the direction of architecture.

The first articulated renderings of this linguistic and conceptual maturity came out of the Memphis experience and they were the various design solutions proposed for the chain of Esprit showrooms in Europe and Asia beginning in 1985. These design projects now spoke an autonomous language, be it about an interior or about external volumes without preexisting inconveniences or restrictions.

SE FOSSI RICCO, MOLTO RICCO, MI CONFRONTEREI CON I MIEI COMPLESSI

33

Ettore Sottsass, <u>If I Were Rich, Very Rich, I Would Face Up to My Neuroses</u>, watercolor on paper, 1976.

Italian Landscapes
Sottsass Associates' Places of Design

Patrizia Ranzo

Italy, for geographical and cultural reasons, has always been a meeting place of cultures and ideas. Here, different visions of the world have confronted and joined one another, generating a varied production of the new.

This land, so permeable and receptive to external ideas and contributions, has combined its readiness to listen with the extraordinary variability of its landscapes, which are the fruit not only of geographic fragmentation, but also of the cultural stratification that has produced them.

Among the characteristics of an Italian identity, in fact, is the idea of nature as product of man's culture—a direct projection of his mental and inner landscape. This link between inner places, the fruit of one's thought, and exterior ones, in a combination of environment, human activity, and the multiplicity of Italian geographies, has generated an openness to dialectics that guides all of Italian culture and its products. Discussing the geography of Italy in this light means talking about its mental latitudes. To analyze the variety of its nature is the same as self-reflection. If we pause longer, then, to observe Italy's physical features and its geographic location, we see that besides its indisputable centrality in the Mediterranean, it also lies slightly to the east. Mediterranean landscapes, especially in the south, are overlapped by those of the east. With such a close interweaving of nature and culture, here even nature is multiethnic. Flowering cacti grow next to olive trees, Arab lemon trees beside hollyhocks, and cypresses next to palm trees. Like all great civilizations, the Italian Mediterranean, in imagination and reality, is inclusive of other cultures. "Athena was black—if you look back—was black," goes a Mediterranean Afro-Neapolitan song, after a famous book. We all recognize ourselves in these remote genetic roots, in this singularly benevolent, variable, fertile, and sometimes harsh physical environment.

In this parallelism of natures and cultures, the Italian identity is reflected before the twentieth century in the intricate fabric of Italian figurative expression. The canvases of its great multiform landscapes, composed of nature, light, and square houses, have told us about our roots. That is when art fulfills the destiny of modernity, abandoning its appointed places to address the streets and objects that accompany human lives. Then the objects become landscapes and possess the colors of the earth, fields, tomatoes, and blue skies. It is in these objects, so laden with meanings and subtle relationships, that we can read our histories and glimpse our inner landscapes. This is why Italian design is so central to our planet's culture.

Ettore Sottsass. Furniture unit in plastic laminate. Gallery Mourmans, 1994.

Unlike northern cultures, where identity is imploded in objects (gray and metallic colors and energetically closed forms), Italian design, especially in its most important facet, is focused on man when history seems to be traveling in an orbit that only tangentially touches our destinies before rapidly disappearing. That facet of Italian design can be identified with Sottsass, for he expresses this multiethnic, dialectic identity—sensitive and ready to listen to even imperceptible signals.

Sottsass is a great designer of inner landscapes in an unbroken cityscape where there is no longer a difference between interior and exterior. He is an obstinate Italian spirit, among the few capable of reading a mysterious inner compass to find their bearings in this changing historic landscape made of concrete, humans, fragments of anthropogenic nature, merchandise, and artificial lights. Through design, Sottsass patiently offers fragments of a vision that would not otherwise be perceived, recovering for us what we absent-mindedly lose daily in this world. Our eyes skim over things without pausing to examine them. "Melancholy" as a positive presence in the work of the greatest Italian designer gives each thing, as it is perceived, meaning in relation to other things. A color, a coffee table glimpsed through a door left ajar, a particular arrangement of flowers in a vase—everything is woven together in a continuous story that accompanies the gestures of his design.

In all these years Ettore has patiently gathered images and has returned them to us after carefully considering possible new interpretations. Thanks to his story, much of our material culture, Italian history and identity—the crossroads between the Mediterranean and the East—will enter the next millennium as the heritage of future generations. Technology, by its very nature, distances us from the world's materiality and from a creative relationship between man and matter. Ettore, on the other hand, maintains a strong connection to the world of things. Technology brings us closer to the universe by making us lighter and by loosening our bonds with the earth. Ettore keeps us firmly on the ground, urging us to look realistically at the things around us. Indeed, this extreme realism characterizes all his work, pushing him to experiment beyond the rigid production mechanisms of the industrial system and to position himself in the small space between man and the artifacts of technology.

All through his life Ettore has often sensed the uneasiness of that "hard white line across the heart"—the slide-rule in the architect's breast pocket—described by Musil at the beginning of this century. The dichotomy between technique and culture—the crux of so many debates on modernity—is simply superseded by a vision of life as a continuous design project. It is from this angle—the only possible one—that a sense of the present, of the contemporary, like a "ghost drifting" through all his oeuvre as an architect-designer, is regained.

Design in the Present

In the roughness of Milan, at times a harsh and inhospitable place, the most authentic spirit of the Italian identity—outgoing and inclusive, lively and open-minded—is physically and mentally represented by Sottsass Associates. The Italian landscape, transferred into the objects and forms of everyday life, finds its historical continuity there, in a continuous and dynamic evolution.

Since the '80s, when Sottsass Associates was founded and the Memphis project—a great electric workshop and condenser of creative energies—came into being, the scene has changed completely, actually demonstrating that the sole constant of these years and of those to come is a continual transition to new states. The transindustrial world, in order to reproduce, needs to continuously define new qualities and goals.

Sottsass Associates operates in this fluid, changeable landscape with design addressed to human beings more than to production systems. Its design seeks, through the world of objects, to always provide new options in a given technological context. Such objects are thus born in the present, as "sensitive forms" situated in space in an active relationship with humankind. It is the quality of this "sensitive interface" that Sottsass Associates' design constantly seeks; it is what emerges forcefully from many of the control systems and machine tools designed in the '80s, from the layouts for an automatic factory, to projects for the corporation Enorme. In these production scenarios, man, expelled from the desertlike spaces of contemporary industry, once again occupies a central position through the identification of new historical qualities.

For everyone in the firm, the work of the '90s has embraced nearly every facet of the industrial world. The universe of color and surfaces, of the objects we all carry around (pens, watches, etc.), of chairs, tables, and lighting, and even of communication—everything has been explored in one continuous design project. During this exploration of the possibilities of contemporary material culture, many staff members have come and gone, while others have been changed by the process. On the threshold of a new century, the whole heritage of that journey begun in the 1950s by Ettore Sottsass has flowed into one major work that is the full and mature expression of Sottsass Associates: the Malpensa 2000 design project.

Arriving at Malpensa from abroad, one immediately feels the Italian atmosphere, composed of "sensoriality, colors, silences, visions, modesties, but also of risk and opulence." Malpensa is a place first, before being an airport; perhaps because it is in these spaces, often conceived to offer a bit of seclusion in a crowded situation, that we travelers can inhabit the swift passing of time. It is "an opaque, inner place," where all the materials in themselves present their warmest and least intrusive aspect. In its simple design, the underlying complexity surfaces only here and there. In this environment the exact will of the architects has been to represent a present very difficult to render: that of our Eastern/Mediterranean Italian identity, the product of so many presents in succession and of the countless minds that have inhabited a civilization as unique as ours.

Ettore Sottsass. Kalligraphy exhibition at the Bruno Bishofberger Gallery, Zürich. 1996.

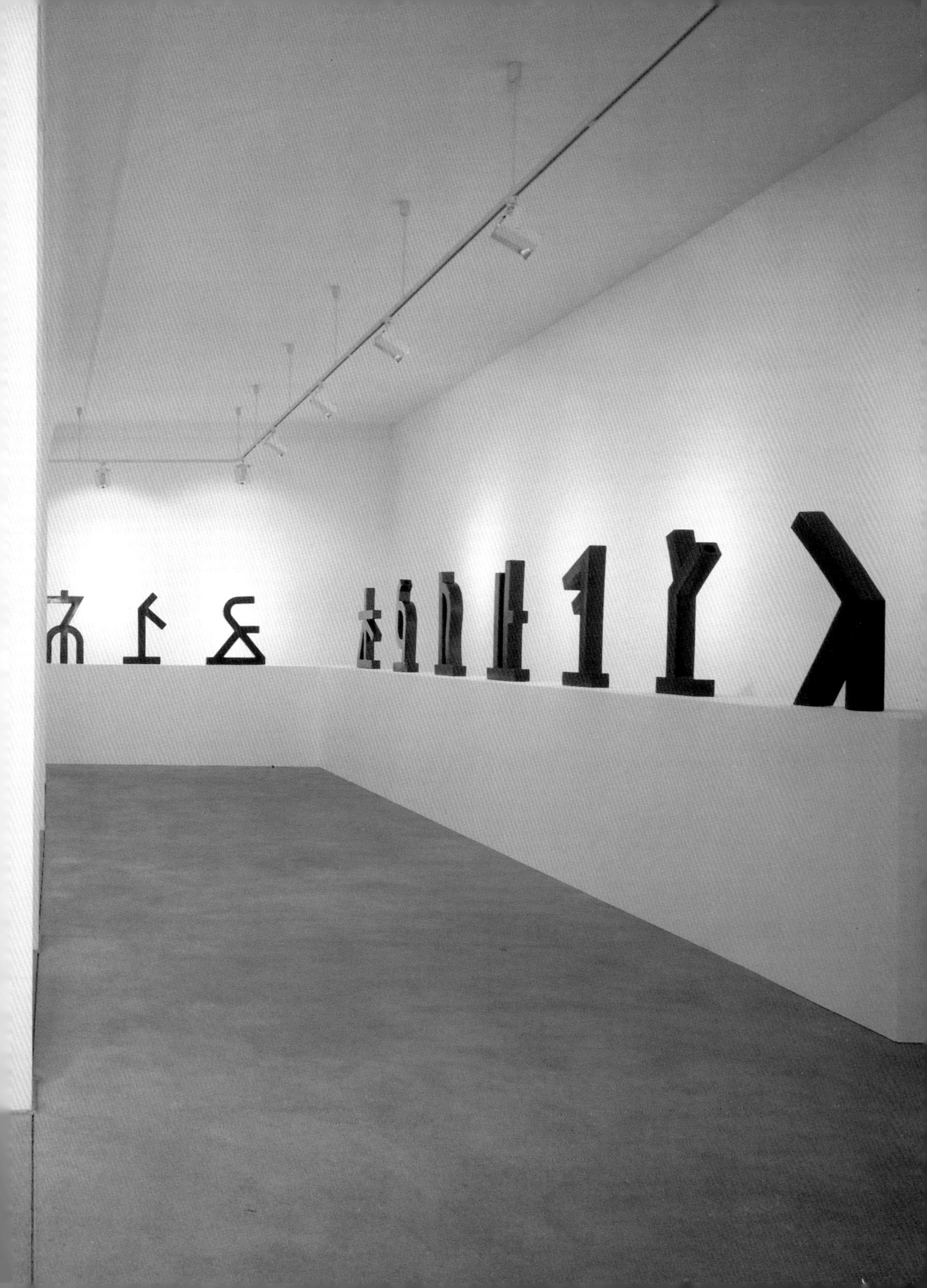

Chronicles of the Beginning

Barbara Radice

They formed a partnership on May 10, 1980, in the small office of a Milanese notary who was a bit surprised to find himself attesting to an architectural partnership made up of, in addition to the famous Ettore Sottsass, two very recent graduates, Marco Zanini and Matteo Thun, "artist" Aldo Cibic, and Marco Marabelli, identified only as "an intellectual." They had only a brief history of meetings and vague understandings in common, but secretly each trusted in the wisdom or enthusiasm of the other, and at least four of the men had their whole lives ahead of them.

The first encounter that eventually led to the partnership was between Zanini and Sottsass in March 1975. Marco, then a second-year architecture student at the University of Florence, had met Sottsass at a workshop run by Global Tools (a free association of radical architects and intellectuals). Later, he had been to see him in his Milan studio and had spent a morning with him. "In those days, Ettore was patient and slow in doing things and had time for others," explains Zanini. Other mornings and afternoons followed, and gradually a warm friendship developed. Their meeting had been a lucky one. The two men, different in age, character, experience, and education, felt a tenuous, mysterious, but extremely powerful bond—that of coming from the same land, indeed from the same "pale mountains," the Dolomites. They also shared certain proud and solitary qualities as intellectuals— optimism, ambition, and the ability to imagine utopias. Perhaps Sottsass was touched to see in Zanini his own anxieties as a young man. Perhaps Zanini saw in that man with his quizzical and detached expression an ideal guiding figure. Then, in 1976, Marco went off to America for a year to "see the world." He wrote letters and postcards and, after returning in 1977, went to work with Sottsass. He graduated the following year, and in 1979 did his military service. From the army he wrote proposals for the future company to Sottsass and to the other aspiring partners who had come onto the scene in the meantime and who were also working with Sottsass in Milan.

Aldo Cibic was a twenty-three-year-old design student in Vicenza in 1978, and the only one in the group to have met Sottsass independently of Zanini, and in completely fortuitous circumstances. A family friend said to him one day, upon discovering that he was studying architecture, "I know an architect too. Do you know him? His name is Sottsass." Cibic knew his name and reputation, so soon after, he, too, was frequenting the Sottsass studio. For two years he commuted between Vicenza and Milan, working at Sottsass's while continuing to do minor interior design jobs in Vicenza. In those years, he drove a playboy's car, a Renault 5, and while in Milan he slept on a sofabed in Thun's living room.

Cibic was patently the opposite of Zanini and also of Sottsass. An extrovert, sociable, and fond of society, where the others were introverted, taciturn, and solitary, but just as ambitious and adventurous, he arrived in Milan and fell immediately into a complicated, insecure, and fairly sophisticated relationship. He admits today that things had looked pretty bleak at times. "I was sure that if I could stick it out, it was going to be the right place," he says, "and I had faith, but the one with the most faith was Ettore."

The beginning with Thun was the most difficult. Thun also was studying architecture in Florence and had had himself introduced to Sottsass by Zanini; but Sottsass was quite "worried" about Thun because "he was making awful things" in ceramics—seagulls in flight and tree-trunks dripping tears and blood. Sottsass was appalled and told him so. Zanini intervened on Thun's behalf. Thun had always lived on the edge of sadism and kitsch, with a stated purpose of "creating a sensation." If it was a sport it had to be the most dangerous—skiing not on snow but on the ashes of a Mediterranean volcano; if it was a vase it had to look like a phallus; and so on. Sottsass's reservations were fairly justified, but in 1978 Thun started to work at the studio. He stayed until 1984, though his focus strayed in 1983 when Sottsass got him a professorship in ceramics in Vienna.

The last partner, Marco Marabelli, also a classmate of Zanini's in Florence, never graduated. Lacking the ambition of the others, he maintained his friendship with Zanini and Thun, but was not as committed to the studio. He departed quietly in 1982, perhaps in search of quieter adventures.

In May 1980, Sottsass was sixty-two years old and everyone, including his future partners, thought that he was quite crazy and utterly irresponsible to form an equal partnership with four nice, intelligent, but totally inexperienced youths. But Sottsass says, "I've always had the idea of working with someone; you can do more things, you can share the effort and the responsibilities. . . . I have always worked with very young people. When I was young nobody gave me any work or opportunities. I knew I could have done outstanding things and I have always remembered that. I also know that people in certain conditions (the problem is to understand the conditions) can do things that nobody would ever have suspected. I believe the young are more honest and sensitive, more questioning and less presumptuous than the old.

"They're not all like that, but . . . those boys looked honest and eager. They were happy young men . . . certainly at the beginning they really were young; every now and then I used to break out in a cold sweat." The studio started like that, on a very adventurous scale. "Even financially," recalls Zanini. "Nobody had any money and we financed ourselves with our first earnings."

Cibic remembers that even the first outside collaborators, "the Mexican gang," reflected the folly of the studio and the mood of the times. "They were four designers from Mexico City. They were all our age—a gang of wild Central Americans. Then came the Austrians and all the others."

By 1983, the studio had already reached a respected professional level and was able to almost double its size. Since then clients, commissions, and collaborators have also been consistently increasing. The graphic design department, launched in 1981 with Christoph Radl, has expanded so much that it has had to move into a separate studio.

The true miracle about Sottsass Associates is the extraordinary understanding that it is not a coincidence but a program well thought out and adhered to day by day with passion. Sottsass Associates even consulted a work psychology specialist in order to better analyze and understand the situation. The fact is that more or less consciously, anyone who joins the group shares its general outlook—a kind of guiding idea for all the work. This guiding idea is the quality of life, one's own and other people's, which each person realizes can be achieved and improved by working well and designing exceptional things. Sottsass says, "We don't see this goal of raising the quality of life as a solitary and personal act. We think the ability to live with others is part of the quality of contemporary life."

The imponderable factor should not be overlooked. "I have a very instinctive blind faith," says Cibic. With a hint of challenge, Zanini adds, "It's a lucky studio," while he adjusts the four orange handkerchiefs in the pocket of his green jacket over a yellow shirt and electric blue tie. "It's like being born handsome; it's luck."

Milan, 1987

Reception Rooms

Herbert Muschamp

We look upon classic Modern design as a reflection of modern industry. Our very use of the term "industrial design" arose, in part, to promote industrial production as an arbiter of aesthetic form in the twentieth century. But in fact the great classic examples of Modern furniture, the chairs and tables of Marcel Breuer, Mies van der Rohe, and Le Corbusier, for example, reflected only one limited segment of the modern industrial system, the factory assembly line.

To the Modernists, the assembly line was far more than a mechanical process. It was also a cultural metaphor—a symbolic rite in which inert material substances were magically transformed into transcendent cultural icons charged with the content of Modern beliefs: the withdrawal of the human hand as an emblem of Romantic individualism and subjective taste; the repudiation of historical styles and their aristocratic associations; the exaltation of the machine as an instrument of social and cultural transformation. Of course, many of the classic Modern objects were themselves not assembly line products; they were hand-crafted works of art that took the assembly line as their subject, objects designed to provide a focus for the rituals through which the world at large would receive the imprint of the Modern vision.

But factory assembly is merely the middle stage of the industrial process—the central panel of a twentieth-century triptych. It is preceded (left panel) by the process of design (including information gathering, or, as it is now termed, "market research"), and followed (right panel) by the process of consumer distribution without which the industrial system could not survive. These two side panels were left blank by the Modern designer. The Modern object— or objet-type as it was called by Le Corbusier and other framers of Modern theory—was [43] conceived to look as though its life as a form began and ended inside the factory walls, as though each chair had been designed by machines and (at least in the view of critics) for machines, without the intervention of human subjectivity. Indeed, in the Modern vision, the object never really did leave the factory at all, for the entire world and all the buildings in it were to be recast in the factory's image.

The world was not, of course, recast in this image, but our conception of "good design" most certainly was, and for this reason it is easy to overlook the inherently modern significance of the work of Ettore Sottsass and the designers associated with him. For on the surface, the designs of Sottsass Associates have repeatedly violated every received expectation of what a work of modern design should be. We see rainbows of color where we expect to see at most a monochrome palette. We see applied surface texture where we expected to see the revealed essence of materials. We see shapes that do not immediately conform to our boilerplate notions of function, and we see surprises where we were told to expect standardization. The easiest way to account for the discrepancy between our expectations and the novel spectacle before us is to interpret Sottsass's work as an irreverent attack upon the Modern vision. The work is irreverent, but it is also an extension of that vision. Nothing in Sottsass's designs fundamentally contradicts the Modernist objective to give visual expression to the cultural primacy of industrialization. Rather, Sottsass has shifted his gaze from the assembly line to the distribution system. His outstanding achievement has been to devise a visual language to express the critical importance of that system in the formation of the contemporary world.

This language speaks of a profound shift in the conception of the modern object from a model of production to a model of reception. Where the production model reinforced values of uniformity, standardization, and objective truth, the reception model emphasizes probabilities, options, and the subjectivity called into play in the act of making, or postponing, choices. This is not the model for which the tool is made or the die is cast, but the model we pinch in the showroom, the model that is one of countless others we thumb through in the catalogue, the one we are allowed to try on for size, or the model of "just looking." Designs by Sottsass Associates are essays in form that take as their subject not the crystallized perfection of the object-type but the variousness and constant change of the context in which manufactured objects take their place and to which they contribute in turn by the pleasure of their company. These designs are not the fruit of a quasi-scientific search for the essential glass or the essential chair, but the findings, rather, of an ambient sensibility that ranges over the field of possible forms and locates in that range a metaphor for the field of freedom.

Freedom, including the freedom to consume, which to those hostile to metaphor may be the only freedom conferred by the machine, is the philosophical imperative behind Sottsass's shift away from the central panel of the industrial triptych. For while granting industrialization its due as a dominant cultural system, Sottsass withholds recognizing the right of the machine to occupy a position of central authority in the spheres of morality, spirituality, or art. Instead, his language declares the power of the internal authority to create its own living space. His furniture, interiors, and graphics offer compressed visual representations of our daily efforts to forge an autonomous passage through the contemporary city—a city seen not nostalgically from the lofty perspective of an omniscient Master Designer but through eyes that migrate without visible logic from the square of grating in the sidewalk to the figure of an approaching stranger, from the glint of an object in a shop window to the rustle of reality in the pages of morning papers. The logic of this scanning is internal. It is not a geometric but rather a narrative structure—the informal structure of ordinary human discourse that we use to say what we did that day, what we witnessed, what we picked out among the universe of choices to fulfill our right to occupy the center of our own universes—to record how we distributed our attention.

It is not difficult to appreciate why the Modernists saw no need to explore the aesthetic implications of distribution. After all, the Modern world was the world to come, the world of the future, the future yet to be built of forms yet to be produced. The Modern priority was to produce the forms that only the future would be prepared to receive.

Sottsass's vision derives from the perception that today, many decades later, we are that future, we inhabit the world, we are on the receiving end of that vision. It is not the world as the Modernists envisioned it—a single window shade of a color not officially approved would have sufficed to ruin that dream—and why should it be? Reception and production are different experiences; why should they look the same? We are not the form givers, we are the form takers. Sottsass stimulates our receptive faculties by objectifying his belief that he and we share the same territory, creating reception rooms even in factories where the whole Modern myth took shape. Who can say that even the machine does not dream of going shopping? Sottsass's abiding aim has been not to remake the world in the image of design but to remake design in the image of the world.

"BARBARIC INTERIOR"

Ettore Sottsass. <u>Barbaric Interior</u>, tempera on paper, 1985.

1980–85

The founding of Sottsass Associates in May 1980 occurred during a time of intense intellectual activity. Sottsass and Michele De Lucchi had been considering leaving the Alchymia group for some time, and in the months that followed, further resolutions were made that culminated, in 1981, in the first Memphis show, which also featured works by Marco Zanini, Aldo Cibic, and Matteo Thun.

Alchymia had represented a major period of research and exchange of ideas. But only two years after the first collaboration of its proponents, differences had begun to appear. Alchymia had never been bothered about sales organization or distribution. Sandro Guerriero, its founder and director, was ideologically very close to Alessandro Mendini and wanted to produce and sell original or numbered pieces that were basically collector's items. Sottsass, De Lucchi, and the other young architects in the Milanese group that had been

taking shape were eager to measure their strength in industry and production in terms of quantity, quality, and image. They felt that the days of radical counterculture and its conceptual theories were over. They were talking about Nuovo Design.

The topics debated were numerous, and concerned not only the compositional and formal part of design, but also more urgent practical matters. In the newly envisioned relations with industry, designers would have their proper say even on marketing decisions; they would not be confined solely to designing objects or furniture to be put into a production line. They would launch a fresh vision of the home, of living, and of relationships with the public.

From the outset, then, Sottsass Associates had to cope with highly complex management problems involving the group's inner relations vis-à-vis the outside. Also at issue were the challenges involved in designing for big industrial companies like Mandelli (machine tools), Brionvega (television sets), or Wella (hairdryers).

From a design point of view, the most important steps concerned the transition to a larger scale, to three-dimensional and inhabited spaces, to the linguistic and formal innovations that had been taking shape during those years at the Memphis shows. The commission for the Esprit shops throughout Europe proved a very important milestone in the evolution of that new idiom. Spaces had to be designed in which people could work, meet, and relax. It was no longer simply a question of making aesthetically pleasing furniture or objects. There was a need to foresee a sensorial interpretation of a complete, liveable space, to invent and utilize a three-dimensional system organized not around the Cartesian plane but around the rhythms of human life. There was an urgent need to study new expressive functions: the use of plastic laminate, asymmetries, the matching of assorted materials, the designing of new decoration, and above all, a wider, more sophisticated exploitation of color, to be applied—precisely—to architecture.

Although Memphis's linguistic innovations had roots in popular tradition, the time had come to put them into practice in zones that in themselves required tighter control and order. The Esprit stores, together with competitions for a multipurpose complex in Hong Kong, for the urban Parc de la Villette in Paris, for the replanning of Piazzale Loreto in Milan, for the Accademia Bridge in Venice, and for the Snaporazz Restaurant in San Francisco, consolidated and clarified the group's outlook on design. They also marked an increasingly decisive and confident approach to and interest in the designing of architecture.

Fiorucci Shops, 1980–83

Designers: Ettore Sottsass, Michele De Lucchi, Aldo Cibic
Collaborator: Anita Bianchetti

In the early 1980s Fiorucci commissioned Sottsass Associates to modernize the image of its shops. For this purpose linguistic elements that had already been identified in the work for Alchymia were applied to the design and were later revived and developed in the Memphis and for the Esprit shops.

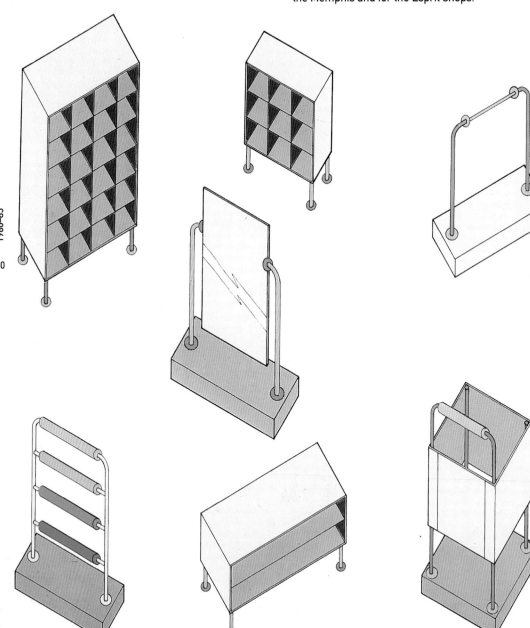

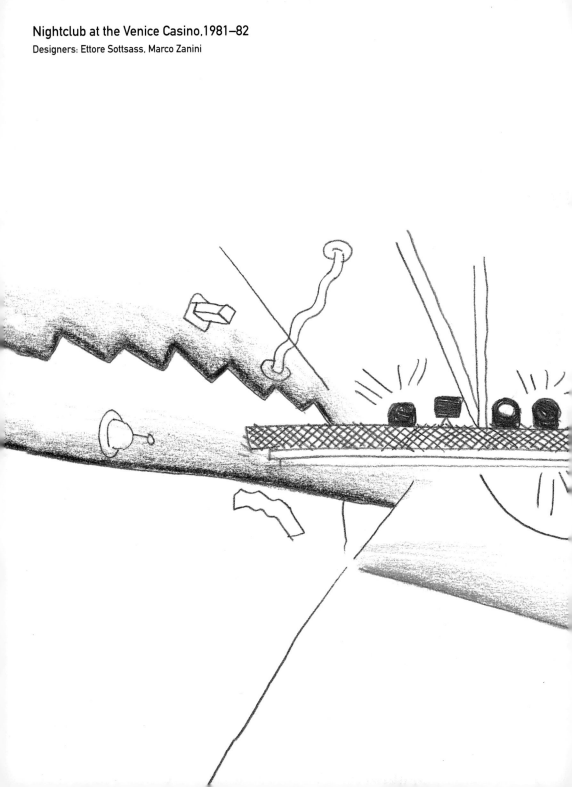

In 1981 the Venice city council announced the restoration of a number of important buildings, including the Palazzo del Cinema, the Casino, and some adjacent restaurants. Sottsass Associates, commissioned to design a nightclub within the casino, proposed a scheme centered around innovative lighting solutions.

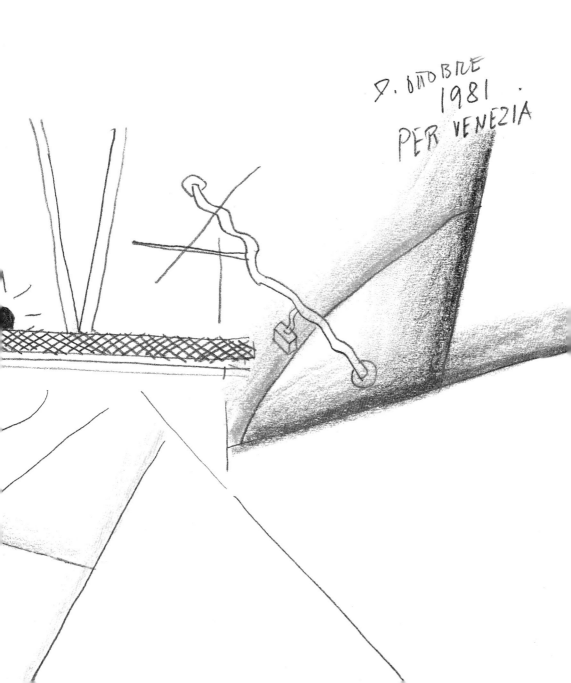

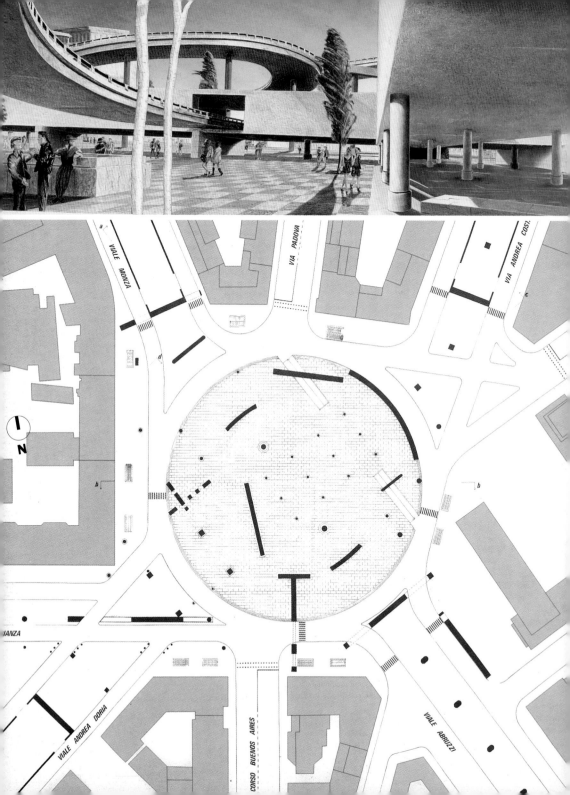

Design for the Redevelopment of Piazzale Loreto, Milan, Italy, 1985

Designers: Ettore Sottsass, Marco Zanini
Collaborator: Giacomo Tedeschi

This design aimed to channel the heavy traffic that converges on Milan's Piazzale Loreto into two routes. The main one, for vehicles entering and exiting the city, is directed onto raised viaducts, while the local route, reserved for pedestrians and for public transport, is planned at ground level. The main streams of traffic intended for the viaducts are channelled into galleries in order to protect the facing buildings against noise, while at the lower level, underneath the viaducts, living spaces have been designed, with shops, restaurants, and waiting areas for public transport.

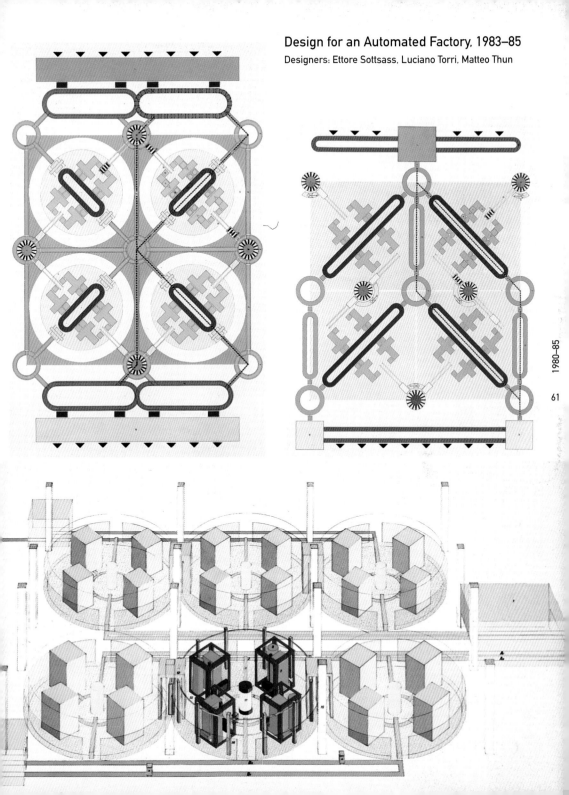

Design for an Automated Factory, 1983–85

Designers: Ettore Sottsass, Luciano Torri, Matteo Thun

Competition for "The Peak" Multipurpose Complex, Hong Kong, 1983

Designers: Ettore Sottsass, Aldo Cibic, Matteo Thun, Marco Zanini

Collaborators: Beppe Caturegli, Giovannella Formica

This international competition was organized by a wealthy Chinese individual who had purchased a large property on this "symbolic" site, which affords an outstanding view of the city and the bay. The program included various types of housing units and a club, restaurants, swimming pool, and communal areas.

The Sottsass proposal centered on having three main blocks, each different in shape but all bearing elements of traditional Chinese architecture, redesigned in a contemporary style. Small, separate blocks house the communal areas. The silhouette of the building on the "Peak" skyline and the extension of the development along the public road that parallels the ridge of the mountain are of particular importance.

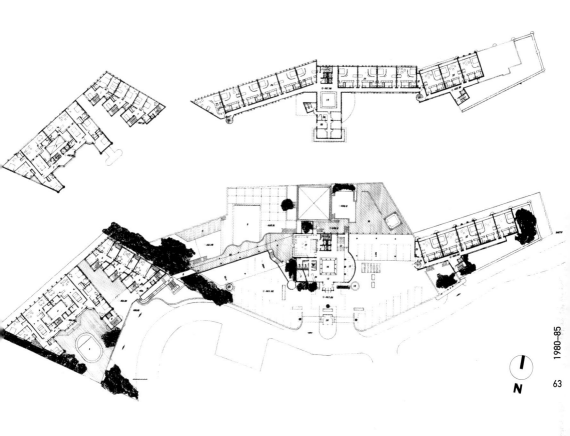

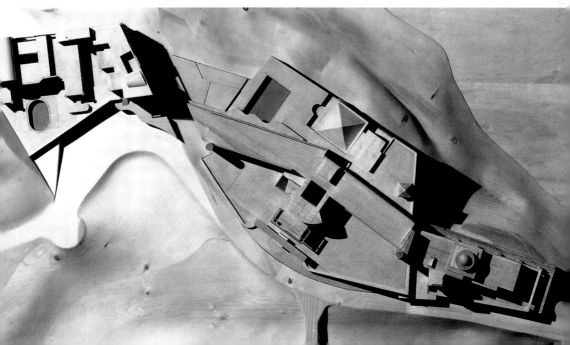

Competition for the Accademia Bridge, Venice, Italy, 1985

Designers: Ettore Sottsass, Marco Zanini
Collaborator: Shaw Nicholls

This design was intended to invoke the great Italian bridge-building tradition, and, more specifically, the design for the Rialto bridge by Palladio. The bridge was envisioned not as a simple means of crossing the waterway, but as an area where the incessant Venetian urban life—from commerce to tourism to socializing—continues, above the water. For this reason the bridge is composed of a series of piazzas, steps, and balconies on both sides and includes covered areas and protected pedestrian lanes.

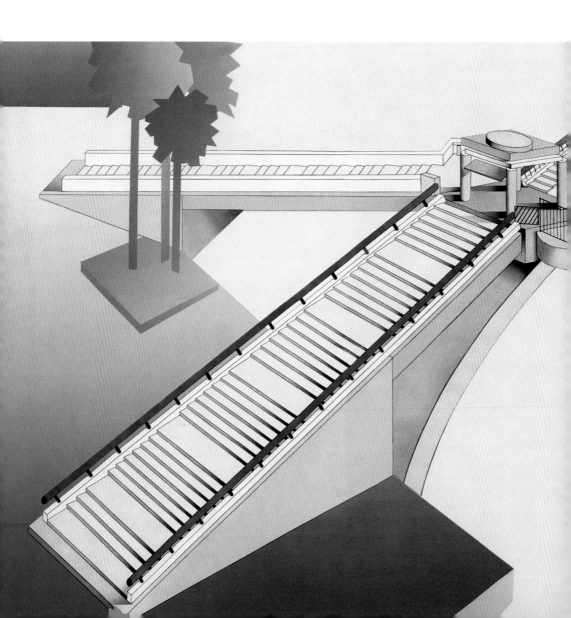

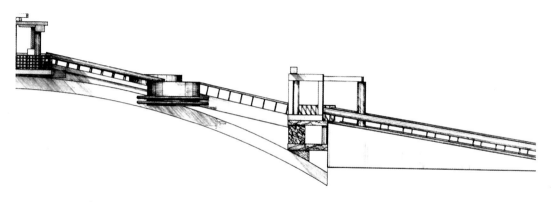

Design for Snaporazz Restaurant, San Francisco, California, 1984–85

Designers: Ettore Sottsass, Marco Zanini
Codesigners: Beppe Caturegli, Giovannella Formica

Snaporazz is the result of an idea by Doug Tompkins. The restaurant, which serves Italian, Chinese, Japanese, and Californian cuisine, was devised as a system of buildings governed by a special relationship between internal areas and gardens. The dining area is divided into different zones, large and small, open or closed. Each room faces a theme garden: the greenhouse with the cactus garden, the tropical garden, the marble garden, and the Zen garden. The bar in the center of the restaurant connects the various sections and provides a meeting place for guests. Above the large restaurant area, which can be accessed by a spiral staircase, a room has been designed to afford guests a view of the bay.

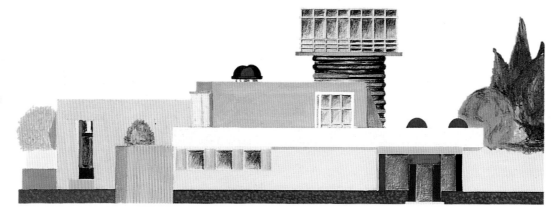

POCO PRIMA ERANO STATI ALLA TORRE. IL MOMENTO MIGLIORE PER STRINGERSI IN UN' ISOLA VUOTA FATTA DI CIELO E DI NUVOLE. MA LOU DISTRATTA DAL CIELO COMINCIÒ A VEDERE GRANDI MERAVIGLIOSE NAVI SPAZIALI E CHIESE DOVE STAVAMO ANDANDO. MOU VOLSE PERPLESSO LO SGUARDO A QUEL CIELO SOLITARIO, MASCHERANDO CON MUGOLII DI FINTO INTERESSE IL DISPIACERE PER L'OCCASIONE PERSA.

SCESI DALLA TORRE GLI SGUARDI DI LOU VAGAVANO ANCORA ASSORTI NEL LOCALE .. SI POSARONO CON MALCELATA SIMPATIA SU UN GIOVANOTTO UBRIACO CHE SI SPENZOLAVA SUL TRAVE CHE PERCORREVA TUTTO L'EDIFICIO. MOU BORBOTTANDO CERCAVA IL SUSHIBAR.

LOU ADORAVA GLI ANGOLI ESOTICI, SOPRATUTTO QUELLI GIAPPONESI, LE PIACEVA GUARDARE, IL CERIMONIALE DELLA PREPARAZIONE DEI PIATTI. MOU DISSE, CON UNA PUNTA DI RABBIA : "NON MI E' MAI PIACIUTO STARE TROPPO IN MEZZO ALLA GENTE".

Esprit Showroom, Hamburg, Germany, 1985–86

Designers: Ettore Sottsass, Aldo Cibic
Associate architect: Dieter Jansen

The Hamburg showroom is located in a very spacious attic on the third floor of a former tobacco factory, situated close to the city center. The main space contains a series of large pillars, painted black or white, that spans its entire length. The salesmen's offices are irregularly divided by partition walls covered in Vicenza stone and gray laminate wainscoting. The colored shelf units that link the partition walls act as portals that announce the entrances to the workstations. Other workspaces are separated by a curved wall covered in large-grain gray wood. Another group of offices, the bathrooms, and the kitchen have been designed as small independent buildings constructed in the clear areas.

Esprit Showroom, Düsseldorf, Germany, 1985–86

Designers: Ettore Sottsass, Aldo Cibic
Project architect: Beppe Caturegli
Associate architect: Herald Syfuss

The 2,400-square-meter Düsseldorf showroom is the largest and most important of the Esprit chain. It even has a bar and a small restaurant. The building is situated in the Düsseldorf suburbs and houses the Esprit design department. A marble entrance has been built over the existing face with columns covered in colored glass tiles. A kind of layering has been achieved, since old structures have been retained and new elements added. The showroom is open-plan with specially researched architectural elements; a bridge dominates the entire space, and the sales area has been defined by a pergola in lacquered iron.

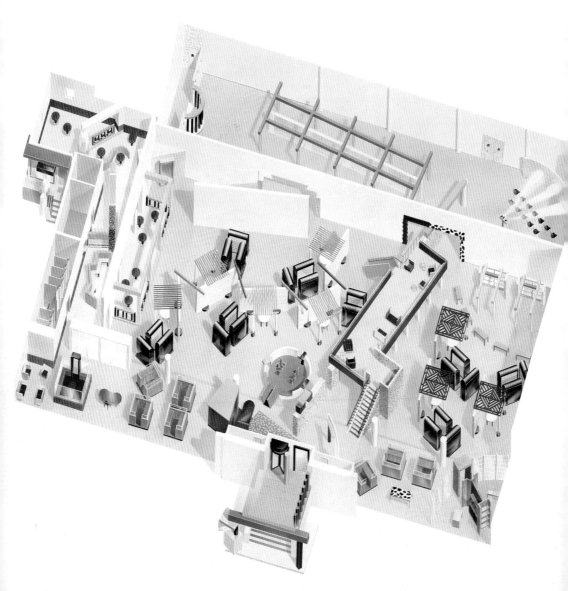

Esprit Showroom, Zurich, Switzerland, 1985–86

Designers: Ettore Sottsass, Aldo Cibic
Collaborators: Shuji Hisada, Johanna Grawunder

The 1,200-square-meter Zurich showroom is situated in a building within the Textile Goods Center, on the outskirts of the city. The predominant elements are the piazza, café, and the large office area. The basic intent of the showroom was to invoke the plan of ancient Italian villages, where a central piazza dominates the town. For this reason the piazza is an enormous space where the main routes meet. The walls, or partitions, separate the "streets" from the "buildings," where business and various other activities are conducted. The reception area, which was built near the garden, is reminiscent of a road in the city that leads to that piazza; here, it is intended for various uses—at times for fashion shows and at other times for business or exhibitions.

Competition for the Urban Design of Parc
de la Villette, Paris, France, 1985–86
Designers: Ettore Sottsass, Marco Zanini, Martine Bedin
Collaborator: Guido Borelli

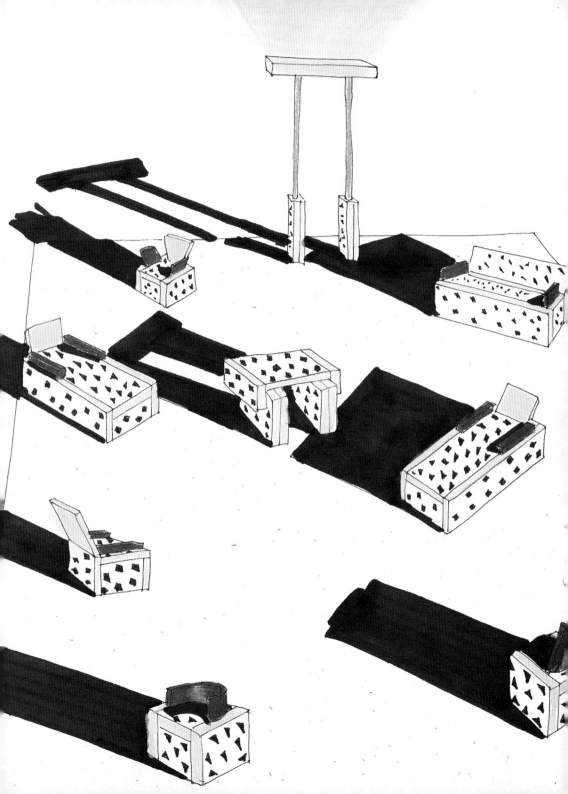

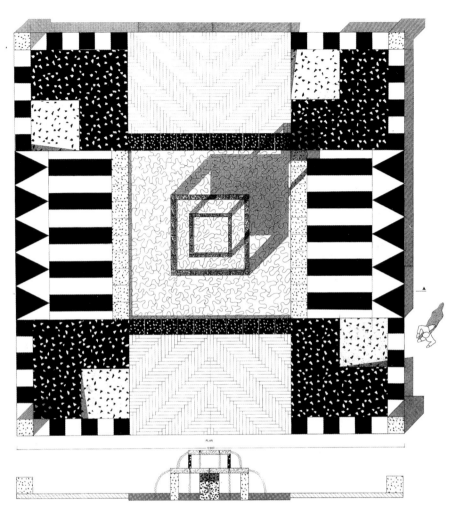

PLAN

12.000

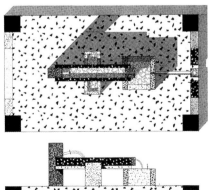

Displays for the Pensieri di Plastica Exhibition, 1985–86

Designers: Ettore Sottsass, Marco Zanini
Project architect: Guido Borelli

CNM Plasma Control Panel for Mandelli, 1981

Designers: Ettore Sottsass, Matteo Thun

CNM Plasma is a modular and numerical microprocessor control system for machine tools. In this design (at left) emphasis was placed on the practical elements of interface in order to simplify the relationship between operator and machine tool. The visual information has been grouped together in the upper part with a vertical reading system that includes a 12-inch screen and a series of indicator lights that show the machine status. The keyboard is divided into functional logic areas made easily recognizable by color grouping.

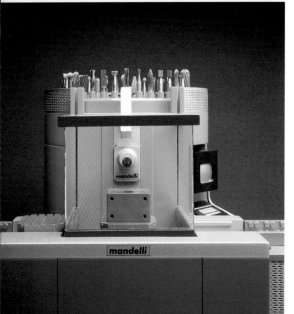

Quasar Machine Tool for Mandelli, 1981

Designers: Ettore Sottsass, Matteo Thun

This tool is a continuous-flow machining center (at left and at right). The design differs from the traditional appearance of machine tools both in the appearance of its external volumes and the organization of the internal parts. As a concept, Quasar is part of a new generation of "friendly machines" that are safer than their predecessors, providing a familiar presence more similar to a piece of home furniture. This design reconsiders the machine as a "module" of a flexible production system, thus enabling its application in various working combinations and fulfilling many production needs.

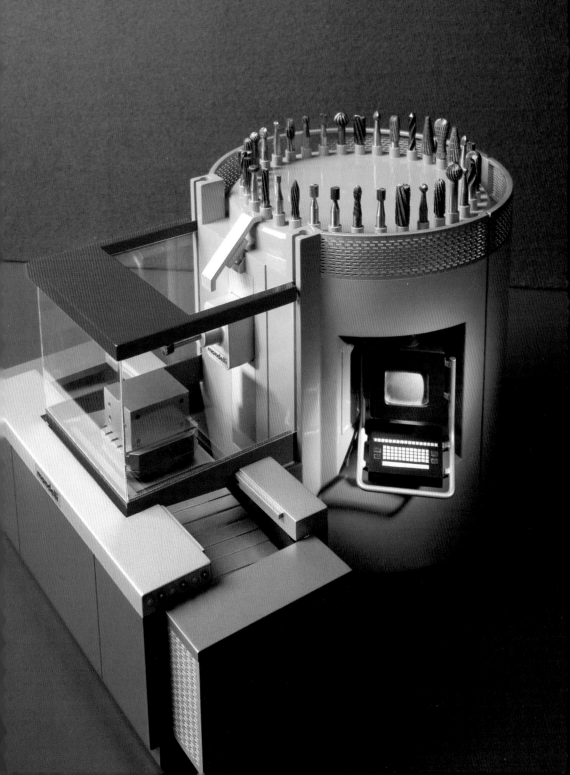

Televisions for Brionvega, 1980–86

Designers: Ettore Sottsass, Matteo Thun, Marco Susani

Work with Brionvega started in 1980 with a project that produced four designs, one of which was manufactured in a limited edition.

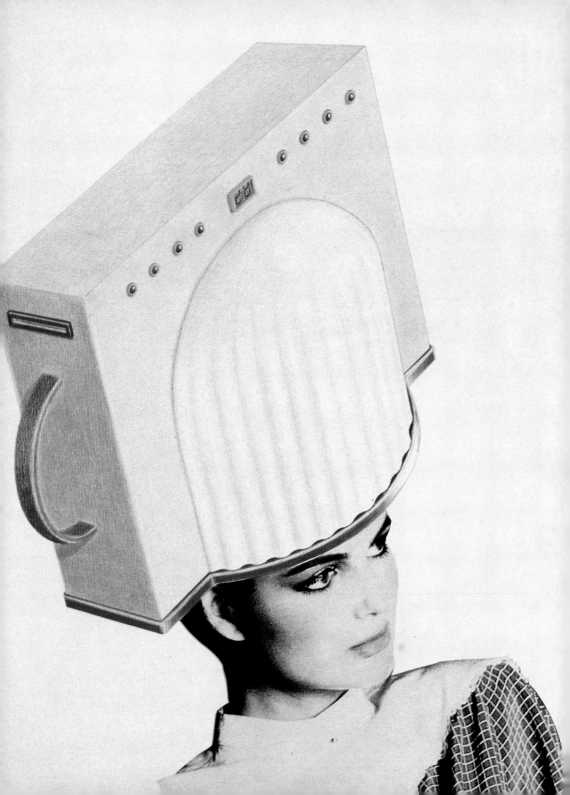

Hairdryer Hood for Wella, 1981
Designers: Ettore Sottsass, Matteo Thun
Collaborator: Theo Gonser

Trace Robot, 1982–83

Designers: Ettore Sottsass, Matteo Thun

Collaborators: Nicola Nicolaidis, Stefano Giovannoni

1986–92

In 1985, when Sottsass had received worldwide acclaim as the charismatic leader of <u>Nuovo Design</u>, he left Memphis and declared his intention to focus almost exclusively on architecture. That same year the studio was joined by Johanna Grawunder and Mike Ryan, two young architects from San Diego who had been working for a year in Florence on a scholarship.

Mattheo Thun had left Sottsass Associates a year before, and in 1989, when Aldo Cibic followed suit, the firm moved onto a different footing. The senior partners, Sottsass and Zanini, were joined by Grawunder and Ryan, who helped direct the architecture department, and by Marco Susani, then director of a course at Domus Academy, who would head the design department. That same year Mario Milizia entered the firm and in 1994 became a full partner and head of the graphics department, just as Susani left and was replaced as partner and head of design by James Irvine, through 1998. In his place, in 1999, Christopher Redfern became the new partner and head of design.

In the meantime the group's new makeup and new goals gradually left Memphis behind, as the firm's unique language began to define itself. In the second half of the 1980s the opening toward architecture and the growing interest shown by Sottsass and the office in this field also found expression outside of Italy. In 1985 Craig Miller, then curator of the Design Department at the Metropolitan Museum of Art in New York, suggested to friend and collector Daniel Wolf that he should get Sottsass to design a large new villa for him on the Colorado plateau. The project, by Sottsass and Grawunder, was the first example in which the linguistic innovations, consolidated through the Memphis and later the Esprit experience, were applied to architecture. Seen in retrospect, Wolf House embodied many of the architectural ideas and themes that were to become increasingly clear and elaborated on in subsequent works: the utmost attention to environment, whereby the exteriors and garden are studied in every detail just as much as the interiors; the care taken with materials and surface finishes; and, above all, the focus on "applied" color. In other words, the project deemphasized abstract material in favor of light and shade and landscape variation as attributes of space and surface design. This idea of architecture as a "place" rather than a monument was to become a key issue in all of the firm's future designs.

Wolf House was followed fairly quickly by other projects: one for a vacation village, again in Colorado; Olabuenaga House, in Maui, Hawaii, which remained in the project stage for a long time but was recently built; the renovation of an old market area in Kuala Lumpur; the MK3 multi-purpose building in Düsseldorf; "Twin Dome City" at Fukuoka; and Cei House, in the Tuscan countryside between Florence and Pisa. The splendid project for Bischofberger House in Apulia, unfortunately not executed, was later "replaced," so to speak, by a different Bischofberger House, built on the hills outside Zurich.

The firm's architectural design continued to be flanked by that of interiors, such as the Alessi shop in central Milan or the Zibibbo bar at Fukuoka, and around 1989 the long collaboration with Zumtobel got under way. The graphic department also was consolidated, until 1987 under the directorship of Christoph Radl, among whose most important works, in addition to all the Alessi graphics and the Olivetti Synthesis catalogue, were the design and layout of the magazine Terrazzo.

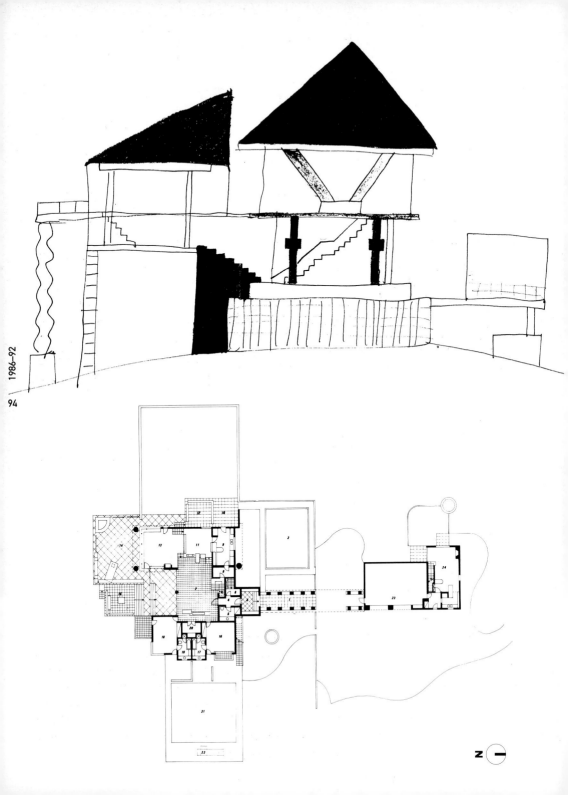

Wolf House, Ridgway, Colorado, 1987–89
Designer: Ettore Sottsass
Project architect: Johanna Grawunder
Local architect: Michael Barber Architecture

Wolf House is a 600-square-meter residence with separate guest accommodations. The project involved design of the building, interiors, and gardens. The main house is organized horizontally and includes two wings linked by a glass atrium that leads to the various rooms. The east wing contains the guest rooms and, on the second floor, a bedroom with bathroom and wardrobe. The west wing houses a second living room, the dining room, the kitchen, and, on the upper floor, a large studio with a library and filing space.

Design for Müller House, Zurich, Switzerland, 1988

Designers: Ettore Sottsass, Johanna Grawunder

Collaborator: Michael Armani

This design brief called for a 600-square-meter single-family house, located in a green and peaceful hilly area a short distance from the center of Zurich. The building's plan, like that of a small village, is organized around a central area: the kitchen. The adjoining spaces are well suited to their various functions: a double-height living room with the traditional saddle roof clad with stone slabs, the block with the double bedroom, children's bedrooms and a library-study that opens onto the living room, and finally a playroom. The lower floor houses the garage and the service facilities.

Design for Village at Log Hill Mesa, Colorado, 1989

Designers: Ettore Sottsass, Johanna Grawunder

The project concerns the design of a low-cost resort village of ten houses, each one measuring 80 to 100 square meters. The various buildings, lined up along a main street, are set back from the road and sheltered by walls. Each house has its own yard with terraces and gardens, and on the rear side the view opens up either toward the valley or toward the Mesa forests.

Design for Bischofberger House, Apulia, Italy, 1988–89

Designers: Ettore Sottsass, Johanna Grawunder

This design brief called for a large house of 1,000 square meters, to be built in Apulia on a site overlooking the sea. The client, an art collector, requested an extensive central space in which to exhibit large paintings, sculptures, and collector's

106

items. The design is laid out around this central area with various rooms, placed adjacent to or supported above the central block, connected to the main room in varying ways. The design then develops outward with terraces, porticoes, courtyards, and gardens.

A second concept, founded on the same basic idea, features continuity of the external surfaces, built, according to the ancient local architectural style, solely in Trani stone.

Design for MK3 Building, Düsseldorf, Germany, 1989

Designers: Ettore Sottsass, Marco Zanini, Johanna Grawunder

Collaborators: Paolo De Lucchi, Roberto Pollastri, Ken Suzuki

The design is for a 26,000-square-meter building situated along the bank of the Rhine. The complex is organized around a central square opening onto the river. The main structure of the building is reminiscent of a table, below and above which the volumes of the residential areas are arranged. On the ground level there are shops, restaurants, a theatre, and a cinema; the middle level holds offices for an advertising agency, office space for rent, an art gallery, and a photographer's studio. The top level, situated on the "table surface," consists of a series of small, lightweight, flexible constructions that house professional studios and offices, and which are laid out like a village, with squares, gardens, and balconies.

MK3 Ideen-Wettbewerb, Düsseldorf
Perspektive des Eingangs von Strassenseite gesehen
Dezember 1989 Sottsass Associati

N

Olabuenaga House, Maui, Hawaii, 1989–97

Designers: Ettore Sottsass

Project Architect: Johanna Grawunder

This 250-square-meter private house is situated on a hill with a view of the ocean. The construction is a series of independent blocks placed under, around, and above a large, black "table" structure. The internal areas are constantly linked, at the various levels, to the external ones, creating unbroken access to the large wooden terrace that overlooks the ocean.

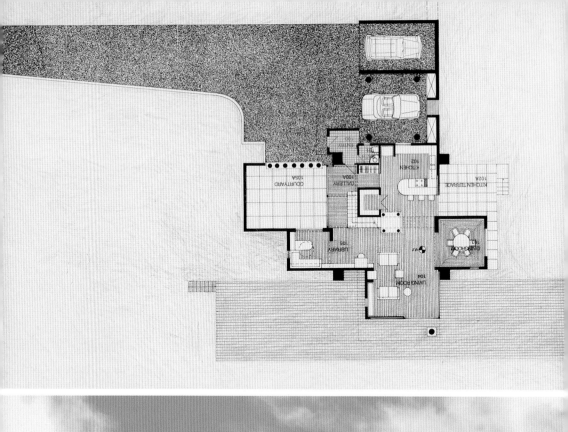

Design for "Central Court" Multipurpose Complex, Kuala Lumpur, Malaysia, 1992

Designers: Ettore Sottsass, Johanna Grawunder

This mall, with shops, bars, restaurants, offices, and a 70-room hotel, is situated in an old working-class district of Kuala Lumpur, between the river and the historic Chinese market. The mall was designed like a village—a self-contained grouping of small structures with terraces and walkways, centered around a large, covered piazza lit by domed skylights.

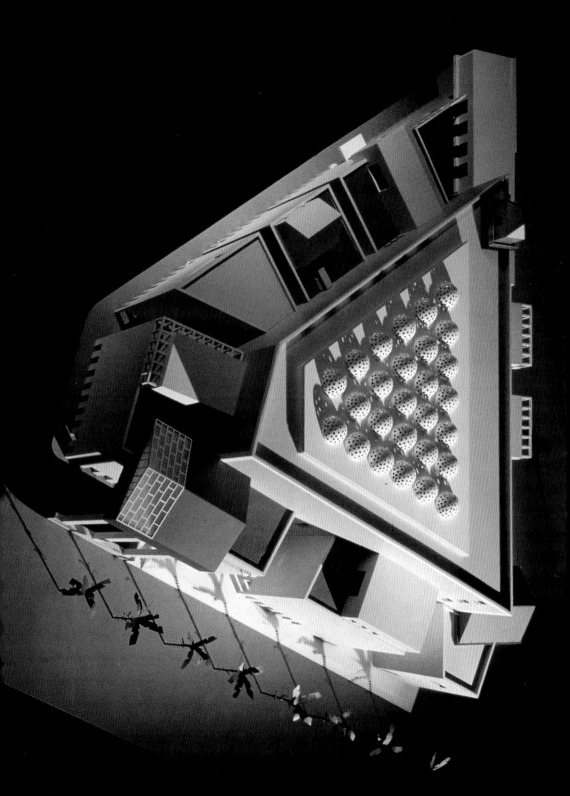

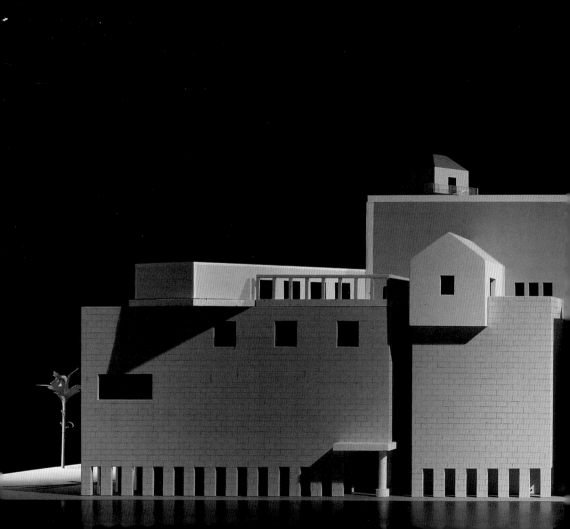

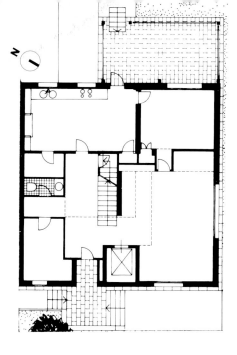

Cei House, Empoli, Italy, 1991–93

Designers: Ettore Sottsass, Marco Zanini, Mike Ryan
Collaborators: Milco Carboni, Tim Power
Local architect: Studio Maestrelli

This 450-square-meter private residence is situated in the Tuscan countryside between Florence and Pisa. The building is composed of a single, two-story block covered in Istria stone, with a saddle roof of red aluminum. The ground floor is used as the day area, with a large, high-ceilinged living room and a spacious kitchen. The second floor holds the three bedrooms, each with its own bathroom, while in the attic the guest room opens onto a large terrace. The natural, diffused lighting comes from a continuous clerestory between the building and the raised roof.

Design for "Twin Dome City" Multipurpose Complex, Fukuoka, Japan, 1991

Designers: Ettore Sottsass, Marco Zanini, Johanna Grawunder
Collaborators: George Scott, Paolo De Lucchi

Part urban planning, part design, this project included an educational-scientific entertainment center, a sports center, and a thousand-room hotel. The design established a relationship between the monumental public areas and the dimension of the visitor by juxtaposing large-scale spaces with more intimate niches, restricted horizons, garden areas, and colonnades. The basic idea was to create a platform ten meters high, covering 90 percent of the potential building area, on which would be situated the three main constructions: the domes of the sports center and the entertainment center, and the hotel. The space beneath the platform was to be used for parking, access, and service. The upper part of the platform would act as a pedestrian zone, with piazzas and gardens far from the traffic.

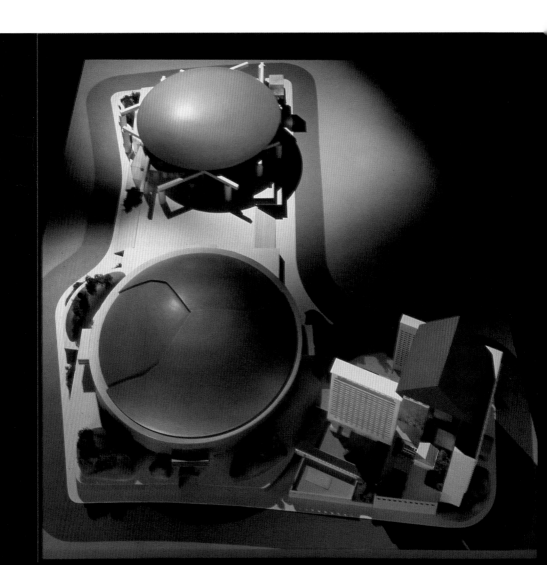

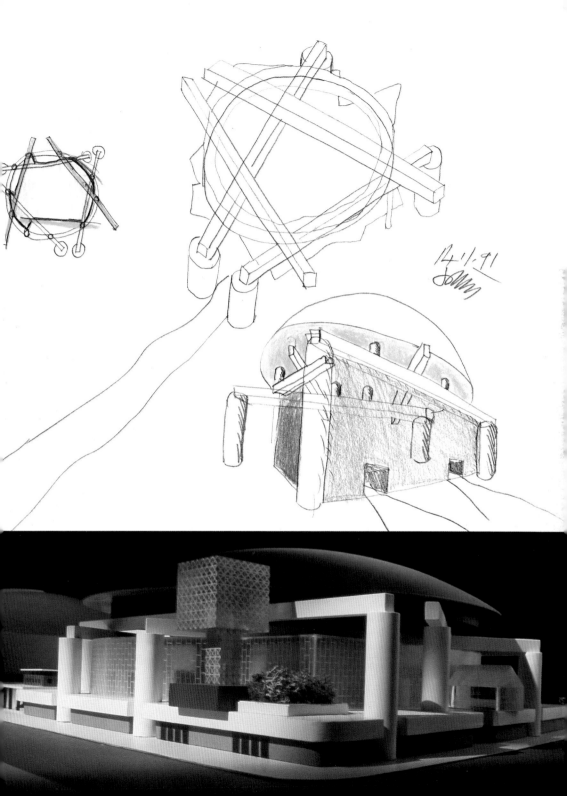

14.11.91

Image for Erg Petroli, 1988–90

Designers: Ettore Sottsass, Marco Zanini

Collaborators: Nathalie Jean, Gianluigi Mutti, Tim Power

Graphic design: Mario Milizia, Douglas Riccardi, Sergio
Menichelli

Erg Petroli commissioned Sottsass Associates to redesign the overall look of their gas stations and the graphic design of their logo, signs, and uniforms. The design exhibits a sophisticated architectural approach to the kiosks and awnings, in contrast with traditional modular, prefabricated units; the plan arranges the various elements of the service station around a small square where drivers can stop and relax.

Zibibbo Bar, Fukuoka, Japan, 1989
Designers: Ettore Sottsass, Marco Zanini, Mike Ryan

Zibibbo, a particularly sweet grape grown in southern Italy, is the name of a bar built in Fukuoka—part of a hotel complex designed by Aldo Rossi. The bar spans various levels, with small rooms, terraces, and stairs that create, in the extremely small space available, a variety of locales: private nooks, open areas, and transit zones. The ceiling is decorated with gold stars on a blue background, like a big sky. Various materials were used, ranging from colored crushed stone in various combinations to white marble to lacquered wood to painted metal. The colors are primary: yellow, dark blue, light blue, white.

Entrance to the Palazzo del Cinema for the 48th Film Festival of the Venice Biennale, 1991

Designer: Johanna Grawunder
Collaborator: Paolo De Lucchi
Graphic design: Mario Milizia

The design for the square in front of the Palazzo del Cinema in Venice is based on the event's logo. A large portal, formed by four concrete-block cubes, supports a trellis that encompasses the logo's luminous eye. The overall effect is that of a billboard in front of the Palazzo del Cinema. The front piazza has been designed as a stone labyrinth, with benches, columns, platforms, and stairs.

Alessi Showroom, Milan, Italy, 1987

Designers: Ettore Sottsass, Marco Zanini, Mike Ryan

The Alessi shop and showroom, located in the center of Milan, occupies three stories, linked by an elevator. The upper floor is used as a showroom, small exhibition hall, and for meetings and presentations; the middle floor has a large shop window overlooking the street; and the basement is used as a sales area and store. The central core of the project is the shop window, based on the design of two large marble display units.

Furniture for Knoll, 1986
Designers: Ettore Sottsass, Marco Zanini
Collaborators: Gerard Taylor, Jorge Vadillo

Telephone for Enorme Corporation, 1986

Designers: Ettore Sottsass, Marco Zanini, Marco Susani
Collaborators: Richard Eisermann, Larry Larsky
Engineering: David Kelley Design

In the early 1980s Sottsass Associates founded, with outside partners, the Enorme Corporation with the aim of designing, developing, producing, and distributing high-tech electronic objects that could express the same figurative force and quality as traditional domestic appliances and objects. The products designed for Enorme include a telephone (distributed in the U.S. and Japan), a calculator, a radio, and a television set.

"Halo Click" Lamps for Philips Italy, 1988

Designers: Ettore Sottsass, Marco Zanini, Marco Susani
Collaborator: Michele Barro

"Halo Click" is a low-cost lighting system for the home, intended for broad distribution in the mass market. The system is based on a standardized light unit that, when attached to different supports, creates various types of lamps. The light unit is engineered to be produced in large quantities. Molded from a plastic material that is resistant to high temperatures, it incorporates a joint that allows the light to be moved into numerous positions.

Lamps for Zumtobel Austria, 1988–98

Designers: Ettore Sottsass, James Irvine, Marco Susani

Collaborators: Richard Eisermann, Riccardo Forti, Flavia
Thumshirn

A ten-year working relationship with the Austrian
company Zumtobel has produced a diverse series of
lamps, created above all for technical lighting. The
latest design, the Aero lamp, uses cutting-edge
technologies specially adapted for work at the
computer.

Above: Artos III halogen lamps; opposite page: ID-S floor lamp.

Aero hanging lamp.

Ciros hanging lamp.

Small Appliances for Bodum, Denmark, 1988–89
Designers: Ettore Sottsass, Marco Susani
Collaborator: Richard Eisermann

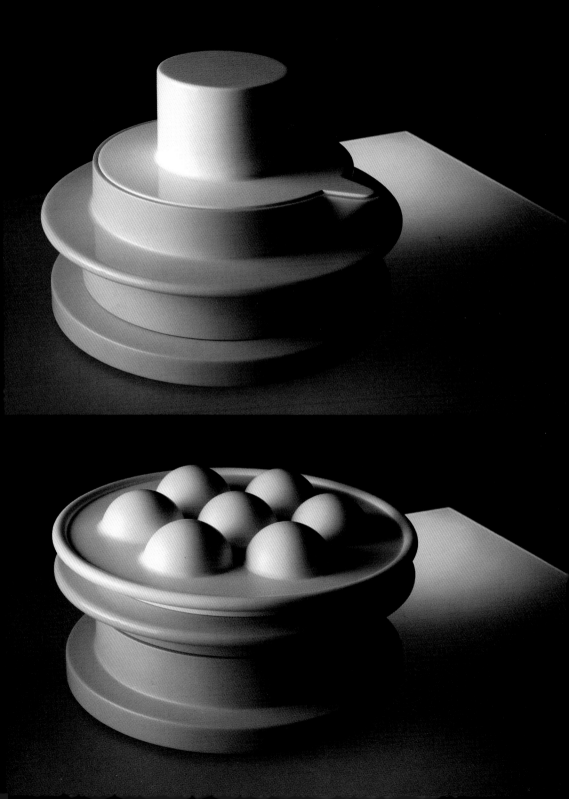

"Toyo Sash" Prefabricated Windows for
Tostem, Japan, 1990

Designers: Ettore Sottsass, Marco Susani
Collaborators: Richard Eisermann, Riccardo Forti

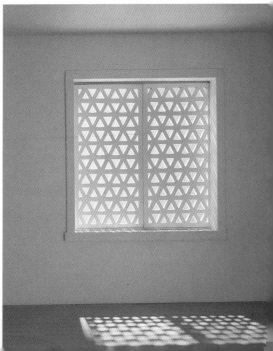

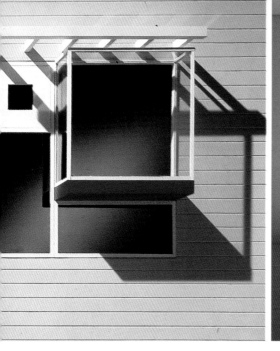

Tostem, the largest manufacturer of window frames in Japan, commissioned Sottsass Associates to design these prefabricated windows for single-family homes.

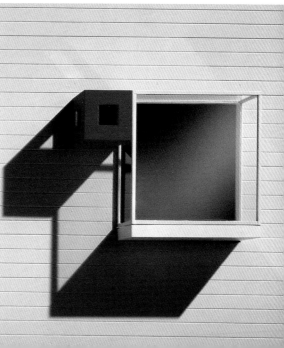

"Angel Note" Telephone Directory for NTT, Japan, 1990

Designers: Ettore Sottsass, Marco Susani
Collaborator: Masafumi Katsukawa
Graphic design: Valentina Hermann

"Angel Note" acts as a personal electronic telephone directory. Linked to the database of the Japanese telephone company, NTT, "Angel Note" allows subscribers to access the central list of phone numbers and addresses and, once connected to a telephone, to dial the number directly. The functions can be extended to transform "Angel Note" into a full-service telecommunications terminal. A hinge with a 180-degree range allows the display position to be adapted to various lighting conditions and the terminal to be used in a vertical position.

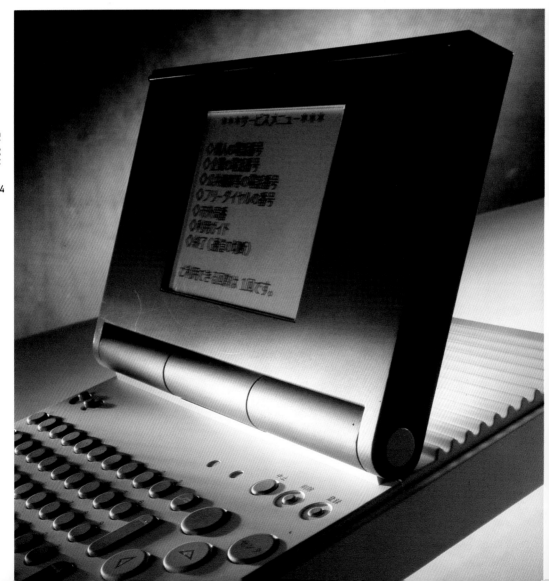

DODICI NUOVI TWELVE NEW

MEMPHIS
MILANO
MOSTRE

Cover for the <u>Twelve New</u> catalogue, Memphis Milano Mostre, 1986 (designers: Christoph Radl, Maria Marta Rey Rosa).

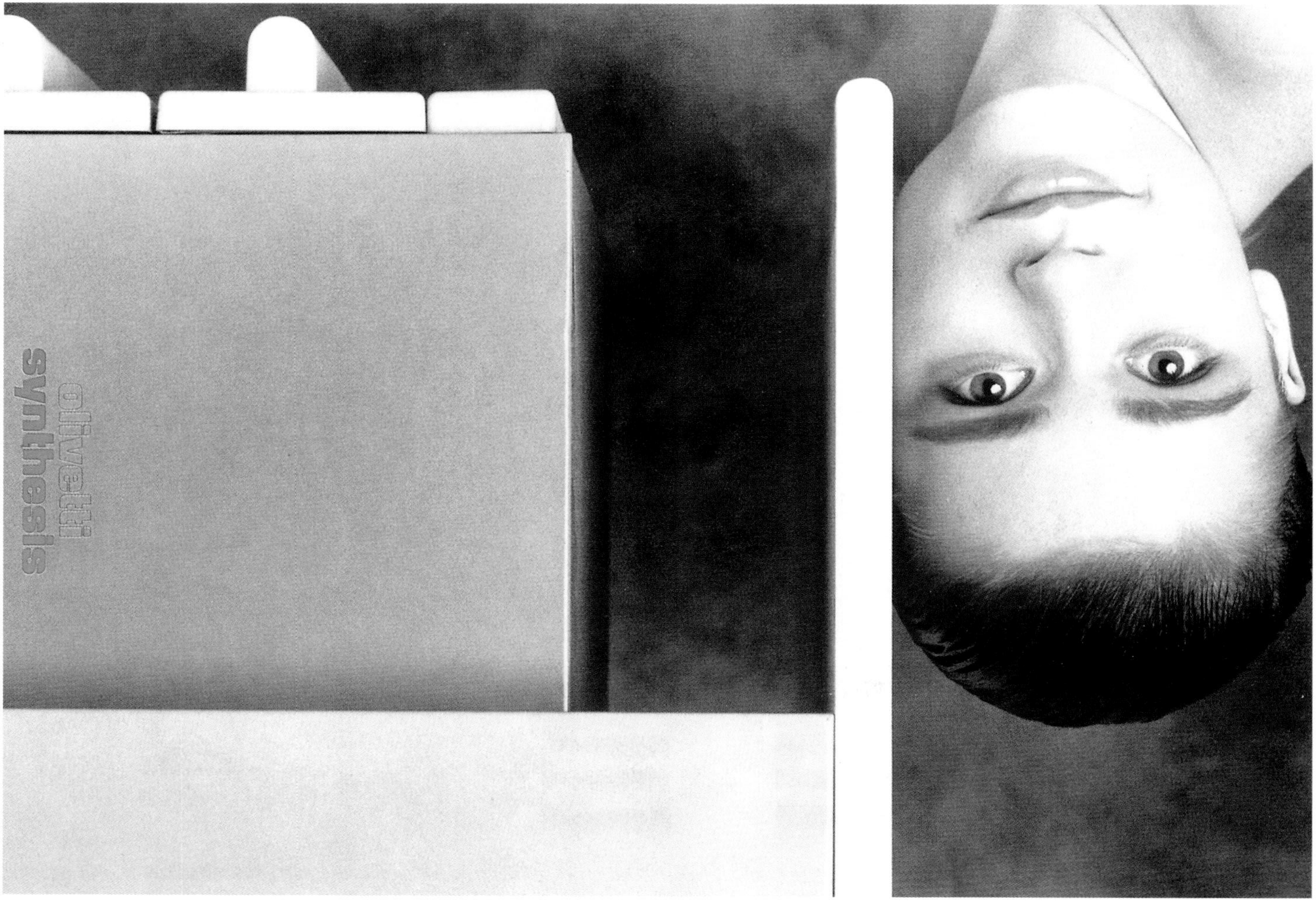
olivetti
synthesis

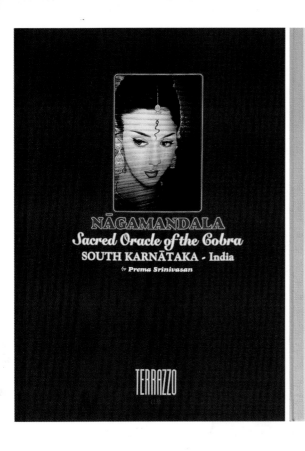

Above: graphic design for the <u>Terrazzo</u> books, 1996–98 (designers: Mario Milizia, Antonella Provasi);
below: graphic design for the magazine <u>Terrazzo</u>, 1989–96 (designers: Christoph Radl, Anna Wagner).

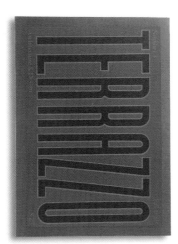

Graphic design for the book <u>Advanced Studies, 1986–90</u> by Ettore Sottsass, 1990 (designer: Mario Milizia).

ERG

1.

ANSALDO

2.

Das europäische Haus

4.

3.

1. Logo for Erg Petroli, 1990 (designer: Douglas Riccardi); 2. Logo for Ansaldo, 1984 (designer: Christoph Radl); 3. Trademark for the design exhibition <u>Das europäische Haus</u>, Germany, 1992 (designer: Mario Milizia); 4. Logo for Ultima Edizione, 1992 (designer: Mario Milizia).

5.

Galleria
delle Idee

6.

7.

8.

5. Logo for the trade fair "Moda Italia," Japan, 1990 (designer: Mario Milizia); 6. Logo for the Galleria delle Idee shops, 1994 (designer: Mario Milizia); 7. Olivetti Design Studio logo, 1994 (designer: Mario Milizia); 8. Trademark for Tessitura Pontelambro, 1991 (designer: Mario Milizia).

XLVIII Mostra internazionale d'Arte Cinematografica - La Biennale di Venezia - Settore Cinema e Televisione - 3/14 Settembre 1991

Above and opposite page: Posters for the 47th and 48th Film Festival of
the Venice Biennale, 1990–91 (designer: Mario Milizia).

1993–99

The 1990s have been a time of expansion and stabilization for Sottsass Associates. The group is more compact, homogeneous, and mature, and its inner relationships are more cohesive and calm. Says Mario Milizia: "There aren't so many stars in the office now, and members are less anxious to make their presence felt. We are quicker now. We have the capacity to take on even very big projects with a relatively limited number of people, and we know how to handle these projects from every point of view: design, graphics, interiors, architecture. All this makes for a special sense of unity. Our language, more sophisticated now, is inevitably more articulate and precise." The firm's orientations, too, are clear. Zanini, who is the only member of the group other than Sottsass to have been a partner since 1980, and who since 1994 has also been the company's managing director, says

he has lost—as is inevitable—a few illusions along the way. He considers it difficult but interesting to keep in step with a perpetually fluctuating market: "To survive we have to accept almost all the jobs offered, which forces us to operate in a lot of very different areas, to be highly flexible, and to create new professional skills. We are, however, very bad at marketing." On the other hand, Zanini says, the group excels in "difficult" commissions calling for cultural sensitivity and flexibility. Sottsass also shares this view. "We are lucky," he says, "because clients come to us knowing who we are: like Zumtobel, Kaldewei, Guzzini, Zanotta, ICF, and Siemens, with whom we have established long-term relationships. Enlightened companies and clients like these are inclined to think of product design as something not confined to sales but which embraces wider functions."

The experience of Sottsass Associates bears this out. In the 1980s, design almost exclusively concerned furniture or products; in the 1990s, there has been an increase in requests for design consultancy on broader and more specific matters, as for instance in the color projects for Siemens, DuPont, or Abet Print. These are nearly always handled by the graphics department, who work in close contact with the others.

As far as architecture is concerned, the prospects are also widening to include briefs for urban planning studies or projects. In their most ambitious form, these concern the designing of entirely new cities, imagined as immense service areas (witness the urban plan for the district of the new Seoul international airport and the plan for the expansion of the city of Inchon, also in South Korea).

Mike Ryan, who with Zanini worked for four years on the new Malpensa airport project, talks about the greater speed and concentration necessary for ever more complex commissions. On the subject of Malpensa, where scale and dealings with public agencies required good management skills, he says: "It wasn't easy, but we succeeded in bringing calm into an environment that is by its nature anything but calm. An airport must be a welcoming place, restful to tired and often bewildered visitors; yet some would like it to be strikingly super-technological and agitated. Designing an airport that can also be 'elegant' seems to be looked upon as a provocation."

A modernity that announces itself in a diminutive and rhetorical way, with high-tech showiness, is a trend to which the whole group seems prepared to concede very little. And yet, due perhaps to the young age of nearly all the partners and staff, the firm is one of the most advanced in the world in terms of technological versatility; it is constantly curious and is committed to invest, materially and psychically, in the most up-to-date design techniques.

Johanna Grawunder has always worked in close collaboration with Sottsass. Asked about the architectural projects executed in the past five years (Yuko House in Tokyo, the Contemporary Furniture Museum in Ravenna, Italy; the Golf Club and Resort in Zhaoqing, China; Van Impe House, St. Lievens Houtem, Belgium; Nanon House, Lanaken, Belgium; and the Birdhouse in Belgium), she says: "Not only have we become much more professional, but with experience we are developing a design style more in keeping with the world today—by tackling problems more realistically. We are equipped also to carry out so-called construction technology projects. We are, for example, working on the integration of light in architecture and have grown more efficient in solving details to meet budget as well as physical and image requirements."

From a formal point of view, the firm's sense of architecture as "place" appears clearer than ever: it is architecture not as a monument or sculpture, not as the brutally minimal technological exploit, but simply as "place" (see the early references in Wolf House), designed around the paths and movements of life, the sum of the fragments into which existence is divided.

"With Ettore," explains Grawunder, "one always starts from the plan by designing the paths of the inner, intimate lives—private or public as they may be—of the people concerned. What happens outside, what will later be seen from the exterior, is an 'accident' produced from the inside."

It is like saying that the outer casing of a structure is not a freestanding shell, but rather that it corresponds to the pulsation of the vital functions inside. It is inner design, not architectonic abstraction; it is "real" architecture.

From its origins in the Memphis group, which was necessarily visually aggressive because it felt bound to promote and exemplify the possibilities of a broader approach to design, Sottsass Associates seems to have gradually reversed itself. The hard side of the project softens and almost vanishes, allowing the fluctuations of its inner complexity, its "software" and vital breathing, to surface. Architecture has become a fluid, iridescent entity, designed from the inside to adapt effortlessly to the incessant metamorphosis of events.

Perhaps, as Mike Ryan imagines, this fluidity is also the fruit of what he calls the firm's "informality." "There is less intimacy than in the past but more naturalness," says Ryan, "Our informality is rare. We tend to project this informal side onto our clients. We try to get them involved, with all due respect, whenever possible." The result is that the projects have a rarely seen depth and transparency.

As far as the partners at Sottsass Associates are concerned, trends are a thing of the past; deconstructivism and dematerialization are finished. It is unnecessary and perhaps even vulgar to formally break down surfaces or volumes. The surfaces and volumes are fragmented and dematerialized naturally. Subdivided by cosmic destiny, they appear and disappear as the mysterious core of our living and being.

Architecture: Constructive Humanism
Andrea Branzi

There is a fundamental difference between the way a designer creates architecture and the way, shall we say, a traditional architect works. The difference lies more in philosophy than in methodology. The traditional architect starts from the idea of the unity of a building—from a certainty that the architectural organism mirrors the unity and self-referentiality of his discipline. In other words, the expressive formula that still governs much of European architecture relates to the world of mechanics. The rotation of masses, the articulation of volumes, and the assemblage of its different parts must at all times guarantee the unity of a structure—in this case the machine—and also its expressive and functional merit. This phenomenological idea always ensures the reconstruction of individual experiences within a preexisting formula of expression.

It is therefore a type of architecture that simulates and stands for itself, confirming its historical mandate as a document whose own logic simulates malaise, values, and enigmas in a literary, metaphorical, and allegorical form. One just has to look at what deconstructivism has become. The movement began with Daniel Libeskind's observation that architecture is thoroughly unfit to exist in the contemporary metropolis (see Archizoom Associates' No-stop City) and in the undefined space of current relational networks. It has become a pure and simple style with which to construct just about anything. Having become a sort of "international" asymmetry, it exorcises the destructuring of logic and design, through a stationary and feasible metaphor having a late-Futurist stamp. Deconstructivism is in fact gaining consensus among the diehards of the traditional academy, now in deep epistemological crisis throughout the West because architecture as a discipline of order is confirmed by this simple asymmetry.

There is, however, a different manner of designing that has a different approach and that can be seen in many design projects and developments of the 1990s. The difference is that the corpus of the discipline—something to be carried out and that connects technologies with semantics and functionality—is no longer evident as a reference.

The idea that there is a cultural sector that comes down to us from history that would even now allow us to recognize architecture, construction, engineering, and design as separate worlds has given way to a wide open field. That field can be traveled in many directions and traversed by a variety of energies and attractions that have no hierarchies or scales.

This type of activity no longer means the joint presence of two or more different disciplines. Rather, it belongs to a design concept that the architect is called upon to express as a transforming and innovative force in the man-made world.

The available technologies are no longer parts of a single cathedral—an icon that validates itself through history. Instead, they are a swarm and a flux that have dispersed, following and endorsing opportunities but not establishing anything. Thus a metropolis is made not of buildings but of places, opportunities (that may also be provisional), relationships, surfaces, and colors that describe a fluid, transferable complex of parts. It never reorganizes itself into a permanent form, but remains an open-ended potentiality. It is an architecture that belongs no longer to the powerful age of mechanics but to the weak energies of electronics. It operates by combining scarcely defined functionalities, striking fictions, and great relational capabilities.

This attitude springs from a straightforward but very new assumption; it affirms that architecture as such no longer exists— only the architect does.

As Ernst Gombrich said, "There really is no such thing as Art. There are only artists." This new approach to architectural design relies on microsystems that fill the generic metropolis of the new millennium—a metropolis devoid of sweeping certainties—but it is animated by a daily, liberal, weak, and incomplete uncertainty.

This is a liberated condition that poses a serious obstacle to the survival of traditional architecture that continues to present itself as a noble witness of time. Instead, it generates another type of architecture that belongs wholly to this time.

The architecture of Ettore Sottsass and Sottsass Associates belongs to this second world, and occupies a precise polarity within it. I would call that polarity Giottoesque, and its beginnings lie in the great originality and stability of a formal logic developed by Sottsass back in the late 1950s that he has maintained since then through constant improvement, development, and variations.

I have often wondered where that logic

comes from, where it gets its extraordinary power, and what this way of designing actually means in how forms are perceived.

Its historical roots are undoubtedly those of European neoplastic culture, made up of an assemblage of simple shapes—cylinders, spheres, planes, and straight lines. On this foundation act the contradictory moods of a search for elementary, almost Jungian archetypes, which Ettore takes from his experience with oriental, Indian, and Japanese cultures, and also from the expressionist edge that is typical of his Austrian roots. Austria has always been the gateway to the East in Europe, and this contradiction is in reality a unity of opposites.

From all this stems Ettore's approach to designing, which does not follow rules of form but pursues instead the assemblage of autonomous figurative elements until he obtains objects or architectures that seem to be the result of a paradoxical, ironic, and desecrating theorem. The result is solid, powerful, and recognizable, but never monumental. If anything, it comes close to the signs of mass culture—to those of Indian temples as well as Walt Disney and, as I was saying, of Giotto. In Giotto's frescoes there is actually no difference between objects and architecture. His buildings are individual elements in a human landscape, on totally equal terms with the figures in the story, a story of human beings.

But Sottsass's theorem is only apparently identifiable with a style. There is in his work a more complex motivation and endeavor which I may call constructive humanism.

This approach springs from a certainty that Ettore has always held rooted in his work. He believes that the vast relational plane that exists between the user and the man-made world must have a formal response: it must respond to the unsatisfied demand for structural archetypes, for decoration, visible signs, and workable systems of logic. For this reason his objects and his architecture are made up of expressive surfaces and recognizable shapes. Indeed, they could be described as globally figurative design that forges ahead without interference, straight from the object to architecture.

This kind of designing must be understood not as a style, but as a response to the important issue of formal quality in the fabricated world. This is no small matter. Indeed, in some ways these issues affect the definition of the whole pattern of development of our society, of man's anthropological equilibrium in a world of advanced technologies. The formal quality of the man-made world is not an optional part of history. It no longer concerns a small minority of people with a discriminating eye, but represents a social issue of broad importance. The formal quality of the world is a major political issue, for this industrial system of ours either will make a formally better world or is doomed to failure.

The recent collapse of socialist countries demonstrates this too—it is no good thinking of creating a socially just (assuming it were) but aesthetically deficient (not to say hideous) world, for this ultimately produces a cultural rejection, which is political as well.

Western morality has taught us that aesthetics is only a minor part of the ethical problem facing humankind, whose salvation lies not in things, but elsewhere, in the kingdoms of heaven. Ancient Japan, by contrast, subscribed to the opposite view—that morality was a small part of a larger aesthetic issue, and that the duty of a religious man was to build the world well. Ettore shares this view.

The world today seems instead to be bent on creating two separate spatial realms, each with its own destiny. One consists of market space, history, violence, and the vulgarity of goods. Doomed to neglect and adrift in a complexity that is no longer a quality but rather the total collapse of order and destiny, it is a world in which only dissociated segments can be designed.

On the other side lies the electronic realm of virtual spaces, dematerialization, and high quality services, where design reigns without let or hindrance in an electronic space where everything is logic and abstract play—an ideal city separate from history.

In the face of this possible (and in part already existing) rift between two worlds, where in the first formal quality is impossible because it is not practicable, and in the second it is useless because it cannot be verified, the search for anthropological identification systems becomes the subject of a possibly dramatic deliberation.

So in Ettore's work the distinctions between an electronic tool, a chair, and great architecture are permanently dropped. These are nothing but outdated categories that fade into a continuous vision of recognizable, friendly, poetic signs, until a physical universe is imagined where the dominant logic is that of man, not of the machine that propagates it. The constructive humanism of this universe is that in which man, the artificial environment, and nature (the world) are saved by beauty.

Yuko House, Tokyo, Japan, 1991–93

Designers: Ettore Sottsass, Johanna Grawunder
Local architect: K3 Institute

This two-story house has an office/showroom on the ground floor. The floor is articulated on the exterior by black granite with a continuous window. It supports a concrete plinth that is the base for the two volumes of the upper floor, which are separated by a small courtyard. The main wing, covered in pink ceramic, houses the guest rooms, the kitchen, and the dining room on the first floor, and a bedroom on the second.

The second volume of the building, intended for the living area, is finished in white-painted plaster and covered by a silver-colored metal roof. A furniture unit, also silver-colored, projects from inside the living area to the outside, becoming part of the building.

Gallery of the Contemporary Furniture Museum, Ravenna, Italy, 1992–93

Designers: Ettore Sottsass, Johanna Grawunder
Project architect: Federica Barbiero
Local architect: Agorà s.n.c.

This gallery, an annex of the existing Contemporary Furniture Museum situated in the Ravenna countryside, covers a surface area of 650 square meters. The center of the design is the tree-filled courtyard, enclosed on three sides by a colonnade of blue contoured concrete blocks and on the fourth side by an industrial-type, prefabricated construction and by a facade covered in mosaic glass that acts as a sign to the gallery. The new construction is linked to the existing building at the ground-floor level by a covered passage and also at the second-floor level by a closed-off bridge. The even, diffused lighting of the interior is provided through a continuous skylight.

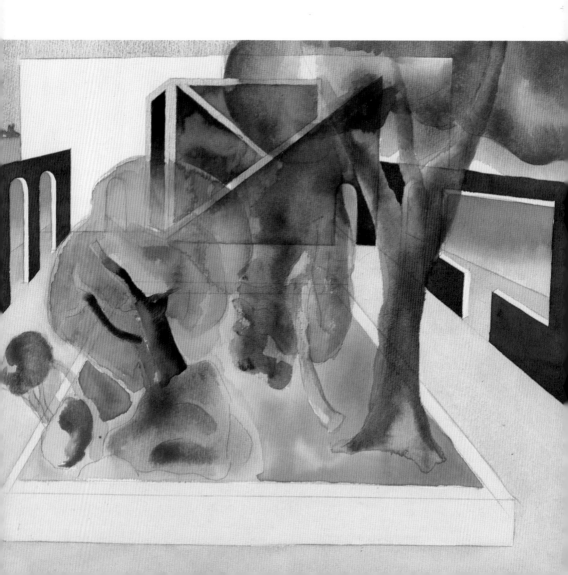

Zhaoqing Golf Club and Resort, Zhaoqing, China, 1994–96

Designers: Ettore Sottsass, Johanna Grawunder
Project architect: Federica Barbiero
Local architect: Design Vision Hong Kong

The 4,000 square meters of this complex encompass a golf club, an indoor gym, three restaurants, and a small, 12-room hotel. Great care was taken in the choice of materials, building techniques, and colors, which all adhered to local traditions. The main block, which includes the entrance, a bar, and the offices, is an open space with roofing in traditional green-enameled terra-cotta tiles and supported by large columns covered in dark green ceramic. A second block, covered in yellow ceramic tiles, houses the restaurants and the gym, along with the showers, sauna, and massage rooms. Nearby stand the hotel and a garage for the small vehicles used on the golf course. This block, covered in red and beige terra-cotta bricks, is linked to the main block by a series of gardens, patios, and colonnades. All the blocks are situated on a single colonnaded plinth of green terra-cotta bricks. Above, access to the various zones of the complex is gained from a large terrace.

Bischofberger House, Zurich, Switzerland, 1991–96

Designers: Ettore Sottsass, Johanna Grawunder
Project architect: Gianluigi Mutti

Commissioned by a gallery owner and his family, this 400-square-meter private house is situated on the hills overlooking Lake Zurich. The building stands on an area originally occupied by a traditional farmhouse

and consists of a main block of three stories that comprise a large living room/gallery, dining room, kitchen, guest room, library, and two large bedrooms. The second block, located near the main volume, encompasses the garages. Both wings of the building are totally covered in slate, except for the part bordering the main entrance, which is covered in Istria stone.

Greer House, London, England, 1993–94

Designers: Ettore Sottsass, Johanna Grawunder
Project architect: Federica Barbiero
Local architect: Gerry Taylor

This project involved the complete remodeling of an eighteenth-century residential building in London. The redesign covered the living room, dining room, entrance, library, study, and stairs area, in addition to the annexed garden. The floors are in red oak, and the walls and ceilings are in plaster.

Ghella House, Rome, Italy, 1993–94

Designer: Ettore Sottsass

Collaborators: Gianluigi Mutti, George Scott

This project called for the redevelopment for residential use of part of a historical building facing the Teatro Marcello in Rome. The apartment covers three floors. The kitchen and main entrance, with direct access from the road, are situated on the ground floor. The second and third floors are similar: both have a day area and a bedroom that can also be used as a study. The unifying element of the design, in contrast with the diversity of the individual spaces, is walnut paneling that covers all the walls of the house up to the height of the windows and down to the oak floors. In some cases the paneling covers built-in elements such as drawers or doors; it also serves to hide most of the utility fixtures installed in the house.

Offices for the Merone Cement Works, Milan, Italy, 1993

Designers: Ettore Sottsass, Johanna Grawunder
Collaborator: Paolo De Lucchi

This design, for the management offices of a cement works in Milan, includes a large open reception area, three offices, a meeting room, and service areas. The central area is designed like a small piazza onto which the private offices of the managers open. The floors of the communal areas are covered in an English carpet with a large floral print.

Amazon Express Motor Yacht, 1994–95

Designers: Ettore Sottsass, Marco Zanini
Naval architect: Espen Øino
Collaborator: Gianluigi Mutti

Amazon Express is a 67-meter, private, transoceanic motor yacht. Originally built as a deep-sea fishing boat by Arsenale Venezia in 1966, it was converted into a motor yacht in two successive renovations in Norway in 1984 and at the Arsenale Venezia in 1994, the latter shown here. The boat can accommodate ten guests in full comfort. The design, conceived with the naval architect Espen Øino, required extensive alterations to the vessel's superstructures and the rebuilding of most of the interiors. The color scheme and the overall image were designed to lend the boat the appearance of both a research vessel and a leisure craft.

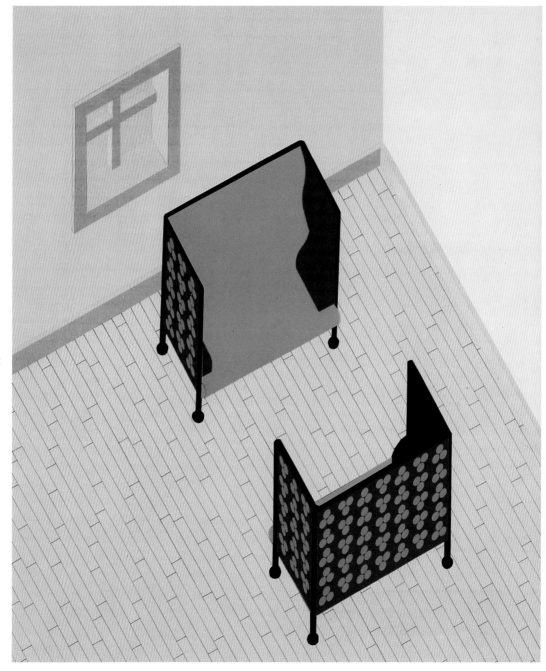

Furniture for Cassina, 1994
Project designers: Ettore Sottsass, Marco Zanini
Collaborator: Richard Eisermann

Zoom Lamp for Candle, 1994
Designers: Ettore Sottsass, James Irvine
Collaborator: Riccardo Forti

Furniture for Fontana Arte, 1992
Designers: Ettore Sottsass, Marco Susani

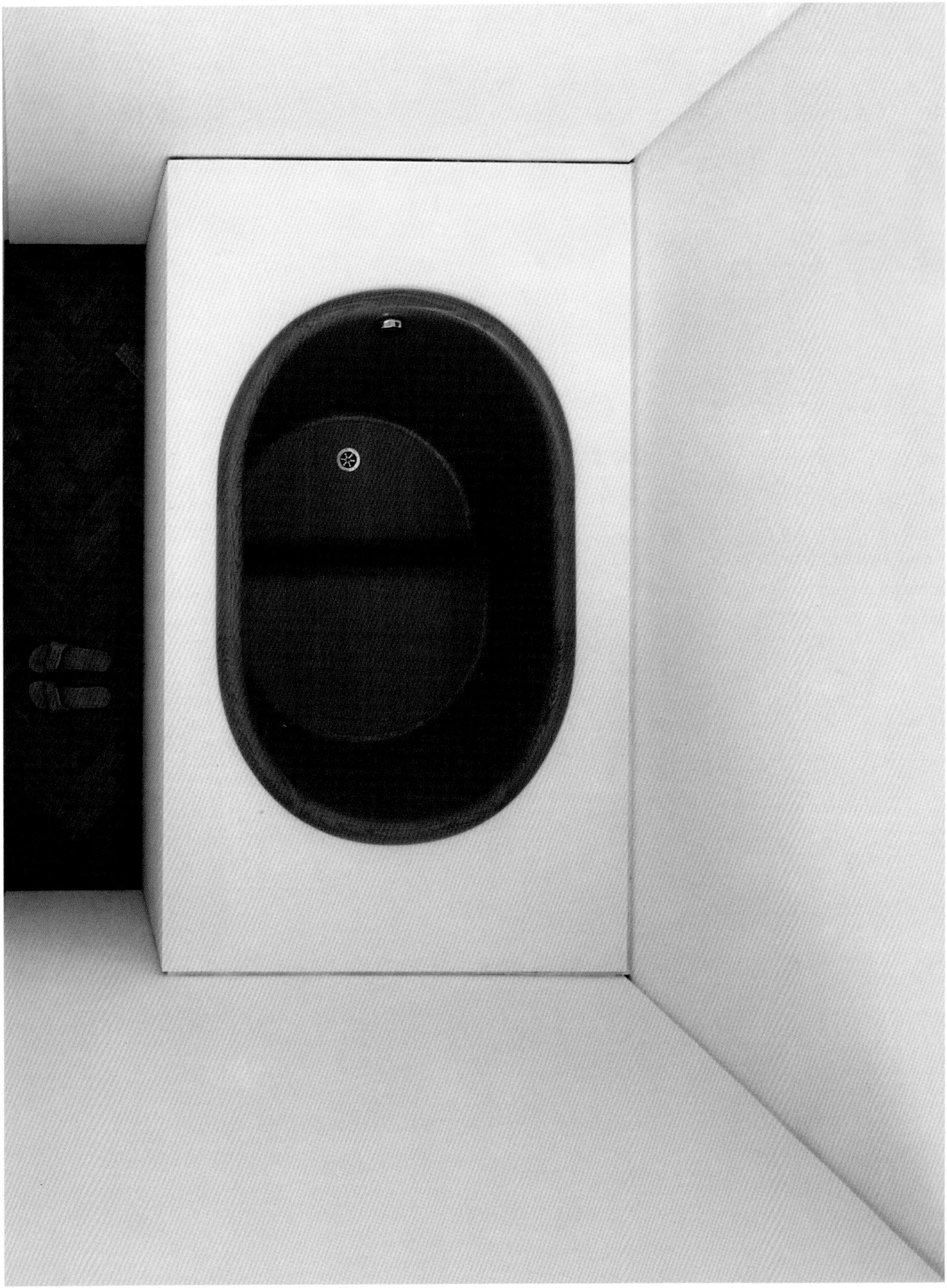

Baths for Kaldewei, 1995–98

Designers: Ettore Sottsass, James Irvine
Design team: Riccardo Forti, Gianluca Giordano,
Catharina Lorenz
Illustration: Barbara Forni

The collaboration of Sottsass Associates and Kaldewei, the leading European maker of steel-molded baths and shower units, aimed to update the design of their products and to introduce a new cultural sensibility in bathroom fixtures.

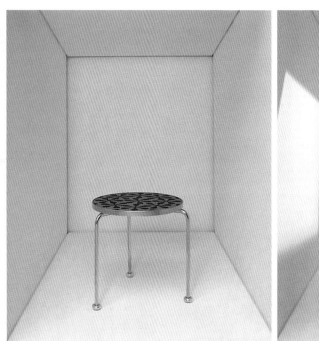

Furniture for Zanotta, 1994

Designers: Ettore Sottsass, Marco Zanini
Collaborator: Richard Eisermann
Decoration: Mario Milizia, Barbara Forni

Designers: Ettore Sottsass, James Irvine
Collaborators: Catharina Lorenz, Fabio Azzolina

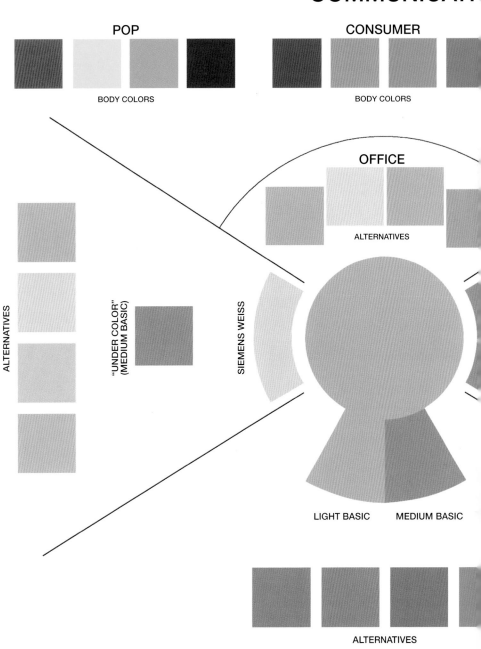

POP

BODY COLORS

CONSUMER

BODY COLORS

OFFICE

ALTERNATIVES

1993–99

222

MEDICAL

ALTERNATIVES

"UNDER COLOR"
(MEDIUM BASIC)

SIEMENS WEISS

LIGHT BASIC   MEDIUM BASIC

ALTERNATIVES

INFORMATICS

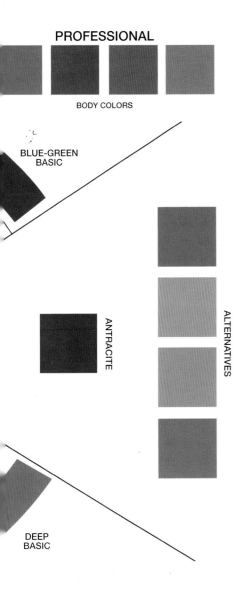

PROFESSIONAL

BODY COLORS

BLUE-GREEN
BASIC

ANTRACITE

ALTERNATIVES

INDUSTRIAL

DEEP
BASIC

Design for the New Colors
of Siemens Products, 1995

Designers: Ettore Sottsass, James Irvine
Collaborator: Cristina Di Carlo

This project required identifying new colors for high-tech products by Siemens. Incorporating the new and growing demands for a warmer and friendlier everyday ambience, a color range was studied that would make the products easily recognizable as members of one of the four product lines: industrial, communications, computer technology, and medicine.

Ettore Sottsass
N⊖TES ON COLOR
edited by Barbara Radice

NOTES ON COLOR	NOTES ON COLOR	NOTES ON COLOR	NOTES ON COLOR	NOTES ON COLOR	NOTES ON COLOR	NOTES ON COLOR	NOTES ON COLOR
Abet Laminati	Abet Laminati	Abet Laminati	Abet Laminati	Abet Laminati	Abet Laminati	Abet Laminati	Abet Laminati

NOTES ON COLOR	NOTES ON COLOR	NOTES ON COLOR	NOTES ON COLOR	NOTES ON COLOR	NOTES ON COLOR	NOTES ON COLOR	NOTES ON COLOR
Abet Laminati	Abet Laminati	Abet Laminati	Abet Laminati	Abet Laminati	Abet Laminati	Abet Laminati	Abet Laminati

NOTES ON COLOR	NOTES ON COLOR	NOTES ON COLOR	NOTES ON COLOR	NOTES ON COLOR	NOTES ON COLOR	NOTES ON COLOR	NOTES ON COLOR
Abet Laminati	Abet Laminati	Abet Laminati	Abet Laminati	Abet Laminati	Abet Laminati	Abet Laminati	Abet Laminati

NOTES ON COLOR	NOTES ON COLOR	NOTES ON COLOR	NOTES ON COLOR	NOTES ON COLOR	NOTES ON COLOR	NOTES ON COLOR	NOTES ON COLOR
Abet Laminati	Abet Laminati	Abet Laminati	Abet Laminati	Abet Laminati	Abet Laminati	Abet Laminati	Abet Laminati

NOTES ON COLOR	NOTES ON COLOR	NOTES ON COLOR	NOTES ON COLOR	NOTES ON COLOR	NOTES ON COLOR	NOTES ON COLOR	NOTES ON COLOR
Abet Laminati	Abet Laminati	Abet Laminati	Abet Laminati	Abet Laminati	Abet Laminati	Abet Laminati	Abet Laminati

NOTES ON COLOR	NOTES ON COLOR	NOTES ON COLOR	NOTES ON COLOR	NOTES ON COLOR	NOTES ON COLOR	NOTES ON COLOR	NOTES ON COLOR
Abet Laminati	Abet Laminati	Abet Laminati	Abet Laminati	Abet Laminati	Abet Laminati	Abet Laminati	Abet Laminati

NOTES ON COLOR	NOTES ON COLOR	NOTES ON COLOR	NOTES ON COLOR	NOTES ON COLOR	NOTES ON COLOR	NOTES ON COLOR	NOTES ON COLOR
Abet Laminati	Abet Laminati	Abet Laminati	Abet Laminati	Abet Laminati	Abet Laminati	Abet Laminati	Abet Laminati

Graphic design for the book <u>Note sul Colore</u> (Notes on color), Abet Laminati, 1994 (designer: Mario Milizia).

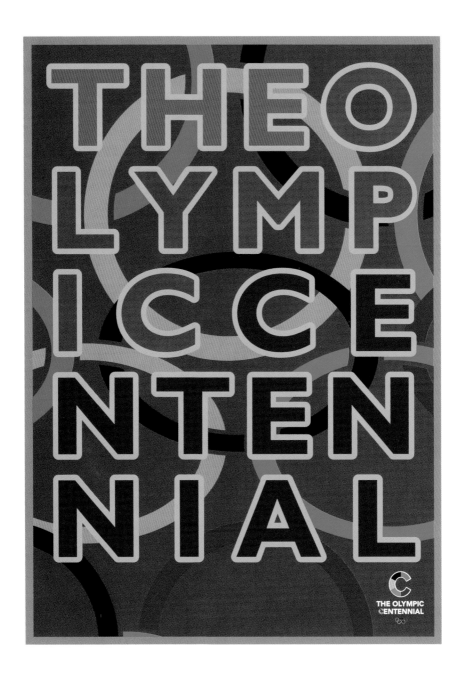

Poster for the celebration of the centennial of the Olympics, 1995 (designer: Mario Milizia).

Poster for the exhibition <u>Ettore Sottsass</u>, Centre Georges Pompidou, Paris, 1994 (designer: Mario Milizia).

Le posate/the cutlery.

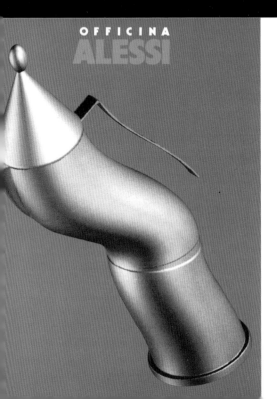

OFFICINA ALESSI

Corporate Identity for Alessi, 1983–98

Designers: Christoph Radl, Mario Milizia, Anna Wagner, Valentina Grego, Costanza Melli

Since 1983 Sottsass Associates has handled Alessi's new corporate identity, including the catalogue designs, packaging, and the photographic art direction for photo presentation, as well as researching the new trademark.

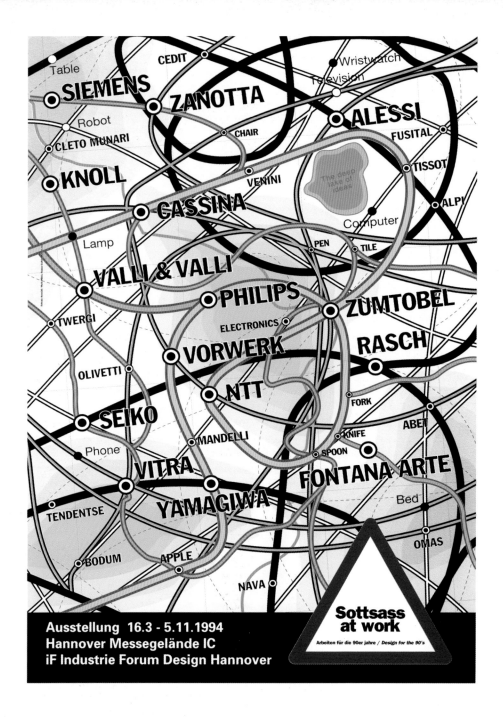

Poster for the exhibition <u>Sottsass at Work</u>, IF Industrie Forum Design, Hannover, Germany, 1994 (designer: Mario Milizia).
Opposite page: Paper bag for the company Uchida Yoko, 1993 (designer: Mario Milizia).

Design for the Seoul Airport Urban Redevelopment Plan, Seoul, South Korea, 1995

Designers: Ettore Sottsass, Marco Zanini, Johanna Grawunder

Collaborators: Oliver Layseca, Elena Cutolo

This project covers a vast zone comprising three mountainous islands, a swath of recovered land between the two main islands, and various land links to the mainland and the city of Inchon.

The development's primary purpose is to house most of the more than 100,000 airport employees and to accommodate airport facilities, but the original idea

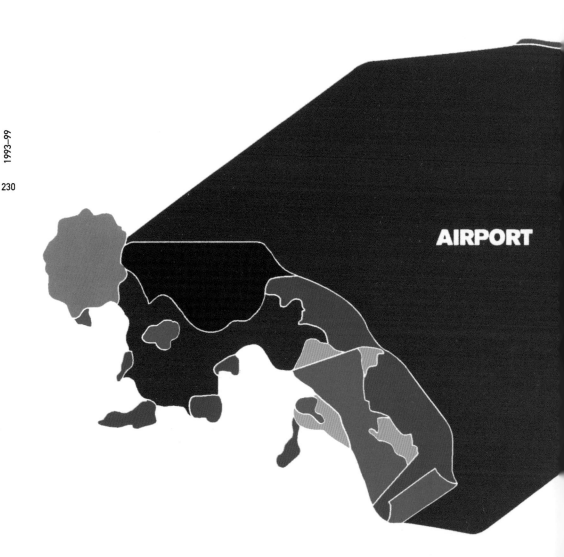

AIRPORT

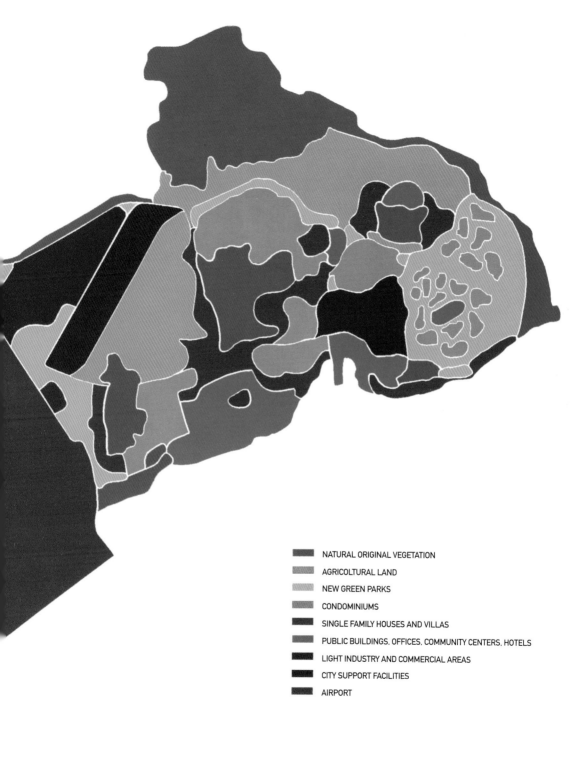

NATURAL ORIGINAL VEGETATION

AGRICOLTURAL LAND

NEW GREEN PARKS

CONDOMINIUMS

SINGLE FAMILY HOUSES AND VILLAS

PUBLIC BUILDINGS, OFFICES, COMMUNITY CENTERS, HOTELS

LIGHT INDUSTRY AND COMMERCIAL AREAS

CITY SUPPORT FACILITIES

AIRPORT

of Professor Kwaak envisioned a semiautonomous territory that would serve as an economic and cultural hub for all of northeast Asia.

Sottsass Associates approached this project with the aim of producing not only a series of designs but, above all, an overarching strategy that would be flexible enough to accommodate all the inevitable changes in the region's social, political, and economic situation, while preserving a basic logic and clarity.

The design contemplates a highly decentralized city in which the location of homes, businesses, production plants, and service facilities would harmonize with the mountainous natural landscape and offer a high quality of life.

An extensive transport system, both intra- and extra-urban, would favor public transport and vehicles with reduced environmental impact. The central concern of the project is the population and its

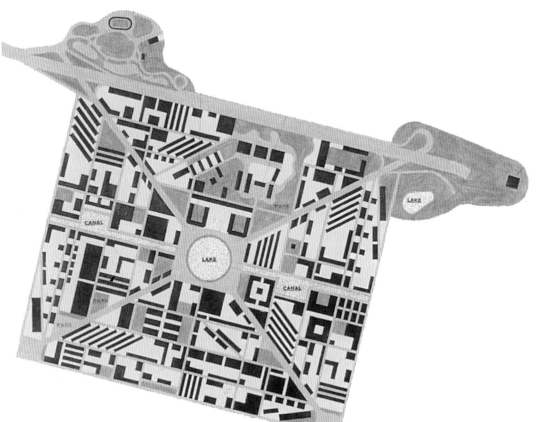

relationship with the town and territory; it is based more on European and Asian models than on that of car-dependent American cities.

A report that Sottsass Associates wrote to accompany the design is as essential as the drawings for understanding the work. It touches on many of the topics that are indispensable to a culture-oriented design for a new city: first, there is the sociopolitical challenge of creating a porous, multicultural hub in a region fraught with political tension; second, there are the purely aesthetic and logistical imperatives of creating an attractive, liveable city that stands in harmony with its unique natural environment.

In the end, the project initiated a productive, far-reaching discussion on new directions in urban planning—and on the successes and failures of the different cultural approaches to urban design.

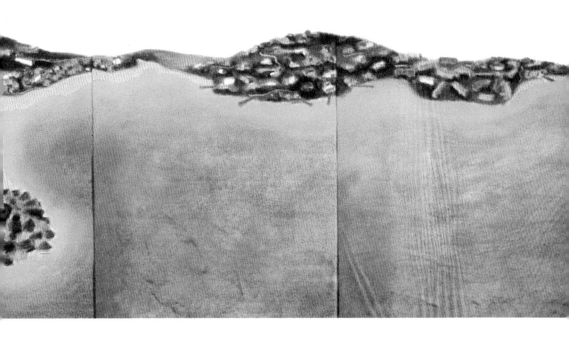

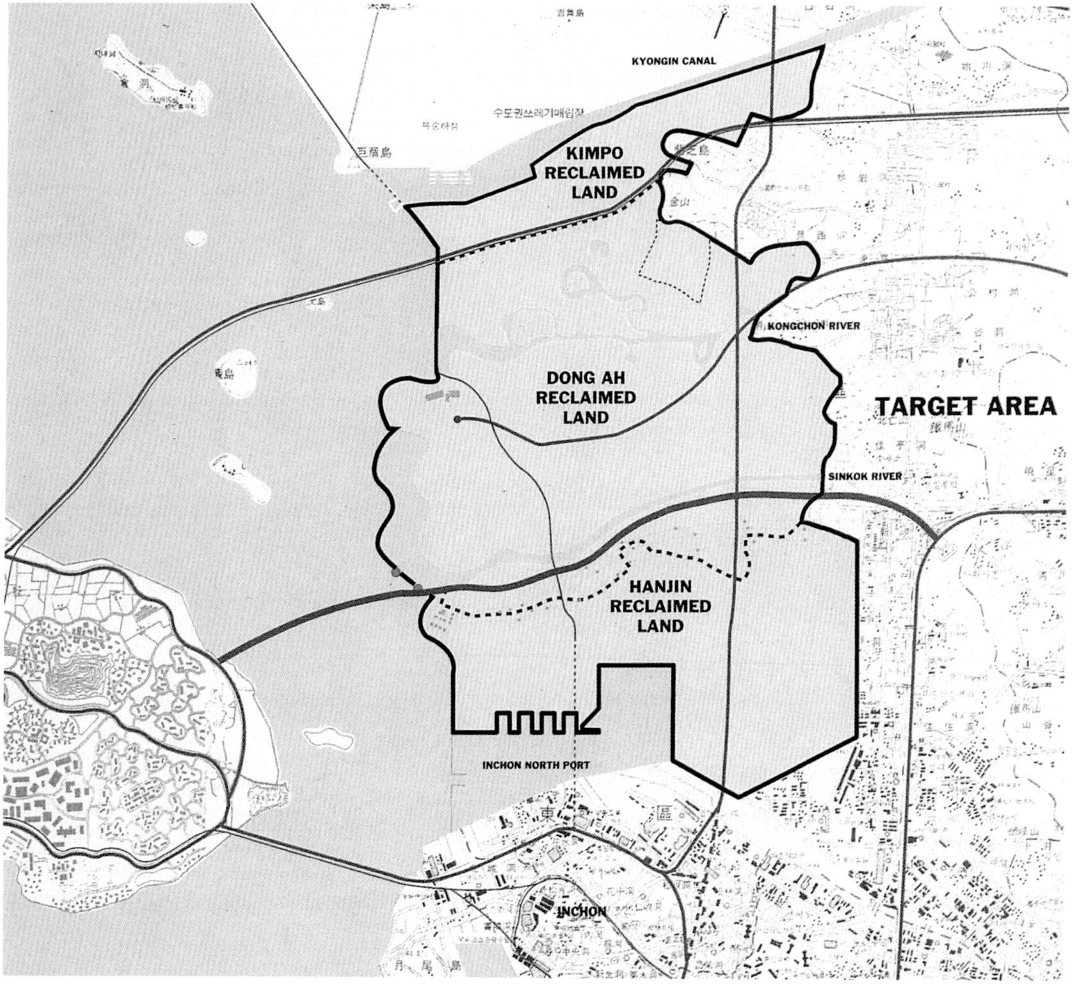

KYONGIN CANAL

KIMPO
RECLAIMED
LAND

KONGCHON RIVER

DONG AH
RECLAIMED
LAND

TARGET AREA

SINKOK RIVER

HANJIN
RECLAIMED
LAND

INCHON NORTH PORT

INCHON

Urban Plan for Expansion, Inchon, South Korea, 1996

Designers: Ettore Sottsass, Marco Zanini, Mike Ryan

Coordination: Milco Carboni

Collaborators: Flavia Alves de Sousa, Bruna Gnocchi, Neven Zoricic

This town-planning project covers 4,500 acres of recovered land near the city of Inchon, approximately 30 kilometers from the capital, Seoul. This area was created by draining the shallow coastal waters of the Yellow Sea with a complex system of dams.

The extension of the city is intended to accommodate 100,000 inhabitants. In addition to defining the residential areas, the proposed plan includes areas for public services, leisure, industry, a new trading port, and the various above- and below-ground transport links between these areas, the nearby international airport, and the cities of Inchon and Seoul.

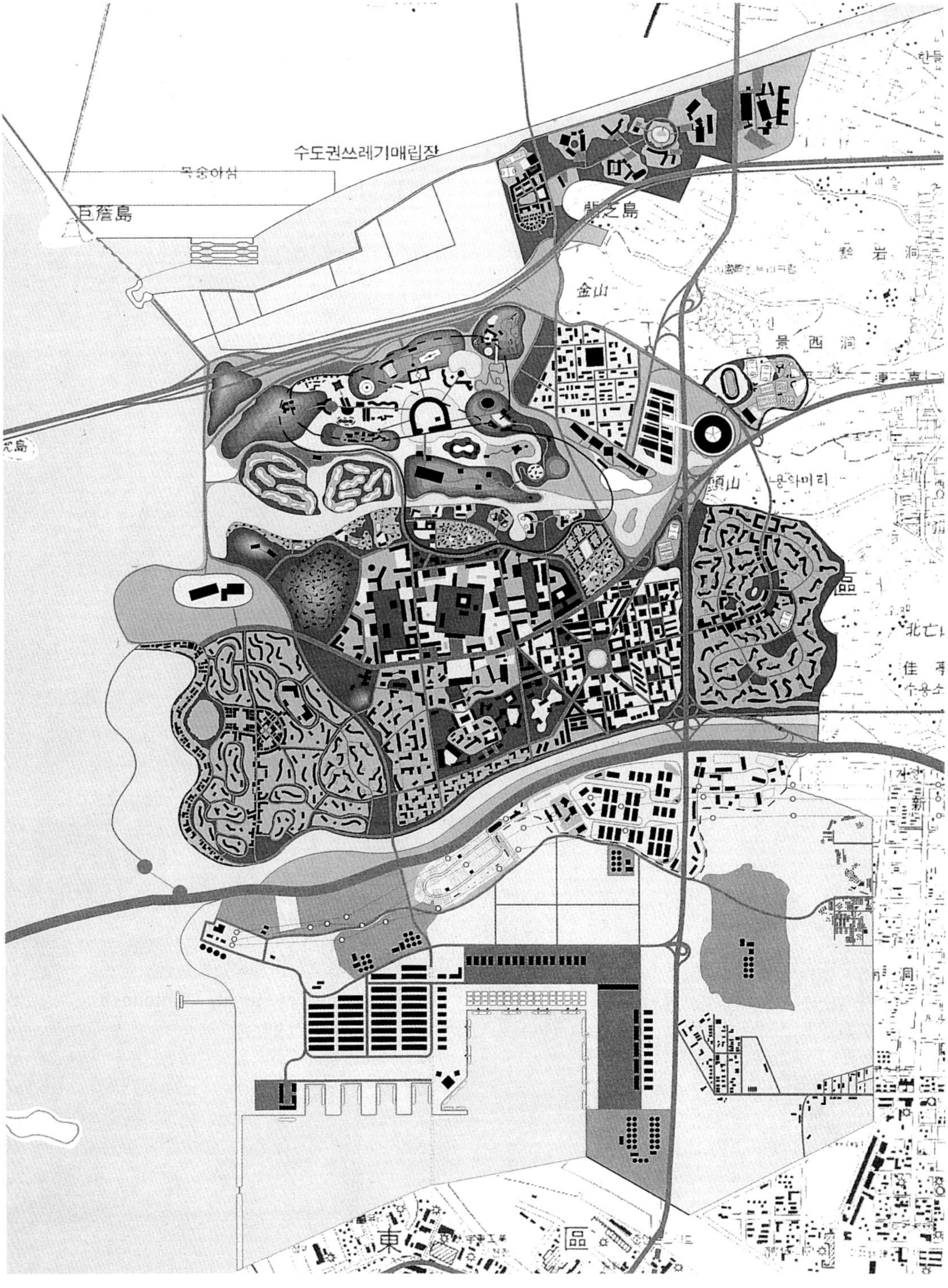

수도권쓰레기매립장

目篠島

金山

景西洞

頭山

北亡

佳

東　　　區

Design for Prefabricated Steel Structures, 1995

Designers: Ettore Sottsass, Marco Zanini, Mike Ryan
Collaborators: Gianluigi Mutti, Oliver Layseca, Neven Zoricic
Coordination: Milco Carboni
Project managers: C.S.M., Rome
Engineering: C.R.E.A., Rome

This research project, promoted and funded by the European Economic Community, studied new solutions concerning the use of steel in the urban habitat. More specifically, the project concerned temporary architecture; it is based on the creation of two structural systems that, when combined, lead to a series of prefabricated steel constructions that would be capable of fulfilling temporary housing needs in parks, at trade fairs, in disused industrial areas, and in zones hit by natural disasters.

The prototypes created with the first type of structure included a small home, a patio, an office, a bus-stop shelter, a bookstall, a shop, a police station, and a covered market. With the second type of structure more elaborate kinds of housing were designed, including single-family homes and multipurpose halls that could be used as civic centers, museums, and auditoriums.

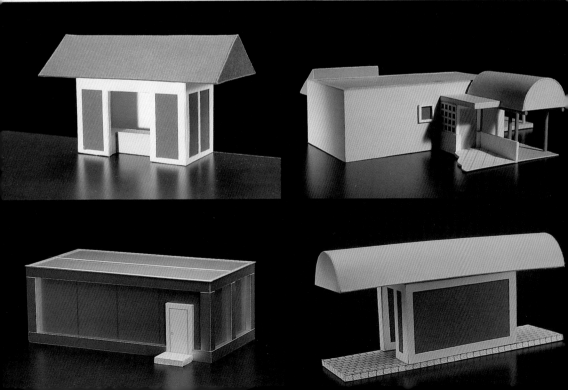

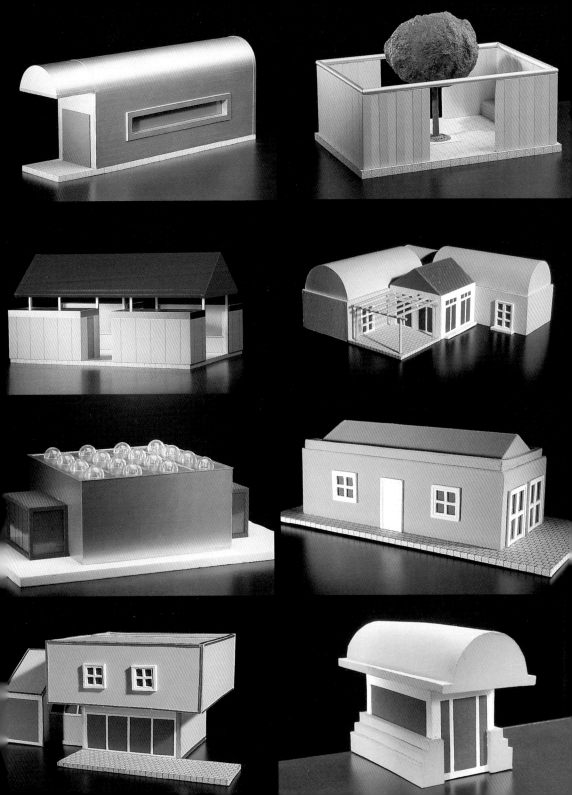

Van Impe House, St. Lievens Houtem, Belgium, 1996–98

Designers: Ettore Sottsass, Johanna Grawunder
Project Architect: Gianluigi Mutti
Local architect: Ron Herremans

This 700-square-meter house, built on a large site flanked by a canal for the owner of a contemporary art gallery, faces the main street of a village in central Belgium. The group of buildings includes the residence, an art gallery, a sculpture park, and a studio for the owner's wife, who is a physiotherapist.

The construction consists of a main wing covered in slabs of blue reset marble hollowed out with the empty spaces of a colonnade and terrace, three blocks covered in white or black stone backing onto the canal, and a vault structure, in ribbed stainless steel, that contains the kitchen, garage, and physiotherapy studio. On the ground floor, the house is divided into two parts by the art gallery: to the east, the two guest rooms and the gallery owner's studio and to the west, the large, high-ceilinged living room and dining area. The two bedrooms, each with a terrace, are on the upper floor.

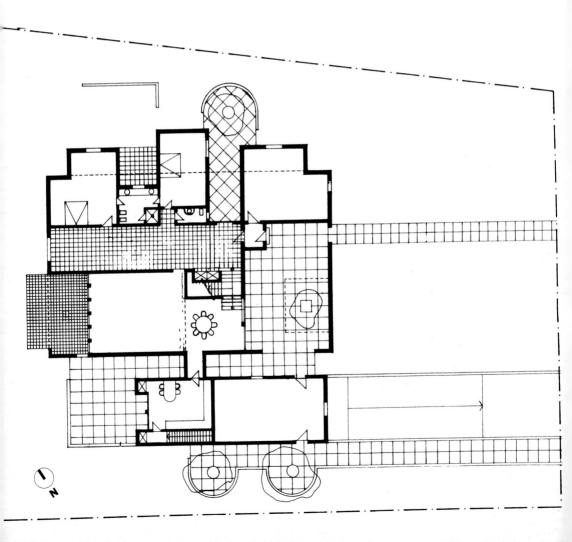

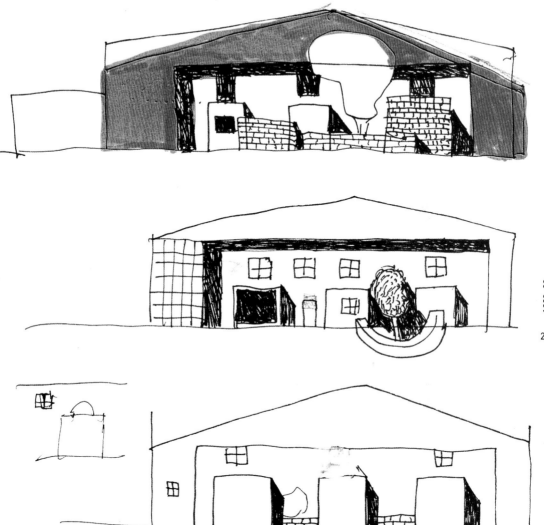

Nanon House, Lanaken, Belgium, 1995–98

Designers: Ettore Sottsass, Johanna Grawunder
Project architect: Oliver Layseca
Consultant: Gallery Mourmans
Local architect: Norbert Foster

This house, built on a large, flat area of land surrounded by tall trees, includes 800 square meters of living area, with three bedrooms (on the second floor), kitchen, dining room, living room, study, and a large central courtyard—in addition to a 500-square-meter space comprising a gym, sauna, and indoor swimming pool.

The interiors, defined by different colors, finishes, and materials, are arrayed around the blue walls of the open inner courtyard, which is accessed via sliding glass doors. The architecture is designed around the routes between structures rather than around the structures themselves. The garden, filled with carefully chosen flowers and trees, is laid out with small courtyards separated by low walls that provide inviting, shaded rest areas.

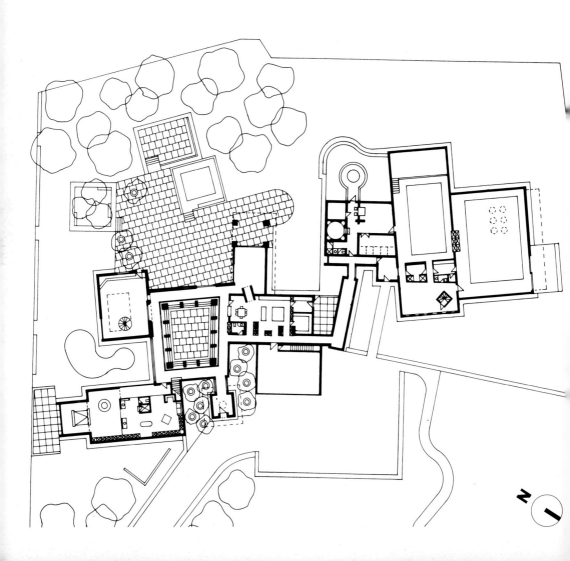

House at Woodside, Palo Alto, California, 1996–98

Designers: Ettore Sottsass, Marco Zanini
Project architect: Oliver Layseca
Local architect: John Barton

This private home, commissioned for the family of a Stanford University professor, was designed to conform gracefully to the tastes and lifestyle of the owners. The house comprises four main buildings.

The living room and dining room, main bedroom and bath, children's area, and study are linked by a central "conservatory." The design also includes a garage and a guest house, equipped with a gym and terrace, that are separate from the main wing. Almost the entire house is located on the ground floor. Special care has been taken in maintaining continuity between internal and external spaces. The home's defining physical features include bricks, roofs in corrugated sheet metal, walls in plaster, and roof tiles in wood.

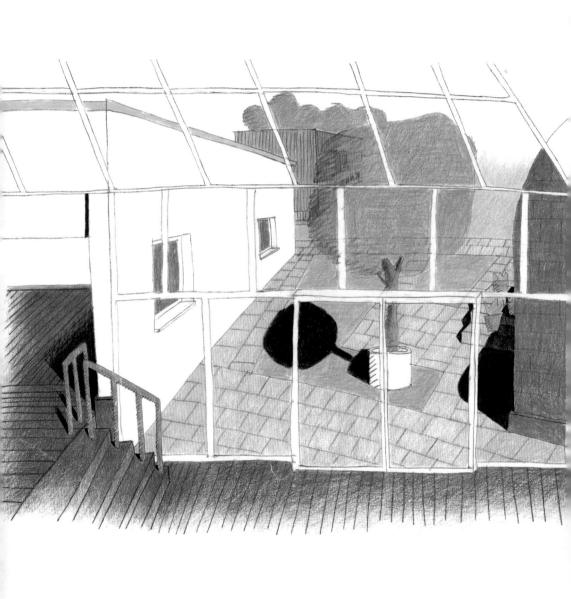

Interiors of Malpensa 2000 Airport, Milan, Italy, 1994–98

In this proposed design, Sottsass Associates set out, first and foremost, to address the complex needs, both physical and psychological, of air travelers. Less imperative were the priorities of public representation, representation of economic powers, or the imagined destinies of the technological future.

Rather than a mechanism or a machine imposed on passengers, this plan envisioned a "place" of human activity—a place in which information is more a suggestion than a directive, in which information serves to accompany and reassure passengers rather than intrude upon them.

To describe the project, the firm often used the phrase "the design of a large opaque interior place." They envisioned a place where the memory returns in some way to ancient everyday Italian and Mediterranean landscapes, in which materials, colors, rhythms, spaces, and proportions respect both the rational, ordered workings of the mind and the vissicitudes of nature.

The design was "opaque" because it eschewed, as much as possible, the presence of shiny surfaces— steel, chrome, plate glass, smooth marble—in order to avoid over-amplified light sources and reflections, which make interpretation of spaces fatiguing for the eyes. Smooth, polished, hard surfaces also reflect and multiply sounds, at times causing acute mental and physical stress. The materials chosen were therefore sound-absorbing, matte stone (not marble), wrinkled laminated plastic, and sound-absorbing plaster, among others.

The design was "opaque" also because it tried to limit the confusing abundance of illuminated information and the superimposing of information upon information. Instead, information was to be limited to that which is necessary and was to be situated only in places where that information in fact "becomes necessary."

To this end, we insisted that information boards be judiciously and regularly spaced, to avoid both graphic and semantic confusion—and to make information easily retrievable; i.e., in an instantly recognizable spot anywhere in the airport. (At one stage in the design we considered greatly reducing the brightness of the signs and creating a hierarchy of light values.)

The overall result is a modern but enlightened approach to space: a simple, peaceful, linear design supported by a range of natural colors—non-chemical, non-TV, non-clinical colors—that have always been a part of the Mediterranean landscape.

The guiding principle of this approach was simple: to communicate to passengers from any part of the world that they have unequivocally arrived in or are soon to leave Italy, not so much via one "style" or another, but through the careful use of the most profound Italian aesthetic—one of senses, colors, and sounds and also of flamboyance and opulence. In the Sottsass vision of the new Milan airport, passengers understand that they are departing from or arriving in an Italy that is not frenetic, not presumptuous, not aggressive, not panicky, but rather an Italy that adopts a culture dedicated to human beings.

Ettore Sottsass, September 1994

Designers: Ettore Sottsass, Marco Zanini, Mike Ryan; general coordination: Milco Carboni; codesigners of interiors: Neven Zoricic, Bruna Gnocchi, Massimo Pertosa; head of design projects: James Irvine; codesigners of design projects: Riccardo Forti, Catharina Lorenz, Cristina Di Carlo; head of signs designers: Mario Milizia; codesigner of signage: Antonella Provasi

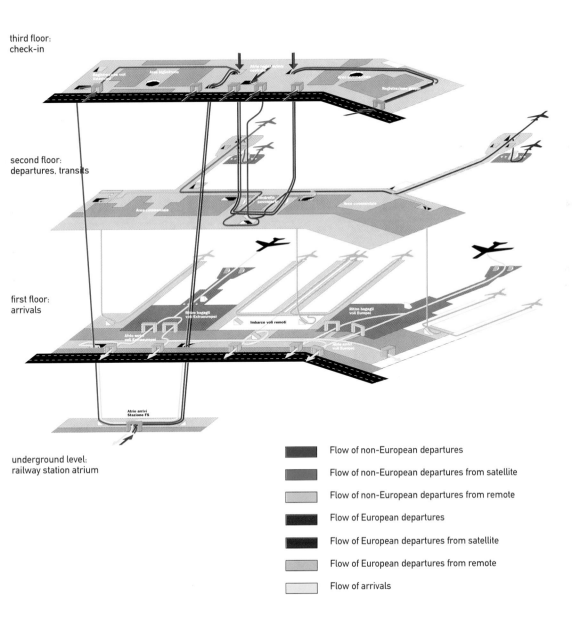

third floor:
check-in

second floor:
departures, transits

first floor:
arrivals

underground level:
railway station atrium

Flow of non-European departures

Flow of non-European departures from satellite

Flow of non-European departures from remote

Flow of European departures

Flow of European departures from satellite

Flow of European departures from remote

Flow of arrivals

Biographies

Ettore Sottsass

Born in Innsbruck, Austria, in 1917, Ettore Sottsass received a degree in architecture from the Turin Politecnico in 1939. In 1947 he set up a firm in Milan where he dealt with architectural and design projects. His design work was collateral, however, to cultural initiatives. He took part in various Triennale exhibitions, and in collective and personal exhibitions in Italy and elsewhere. He played an international role in innovating design in the pre- and postwar years.

In 1958 he started to work with Olivetti as a design consultant. In 1959 he designed, among other things, the first Italian electronic calculator and, later, various peripheral calculation systems, as well as typewriter models such as Praxis, Tekne, Editor, and Valentine. A Valentine typewriter is now included in the permanent collection at New York's Museum of Modern Art.

After a long lecture tour of British universities, Sottsass was awarded an honorary degree by the Royal College of Art in London. In 1980 he founded the firm Sottsass Associates, where he continued his work as architect and designer. The following year he set up, with colleagues, friends, and internationally renowned architects, the Memphis group, which soon became the flagship of "new design" and a landmark for the contemporary avant-garde movement. His works became part of the permanent collections of important museums in major cities: New York, Paris, Sidney, Denver, Stockholm, London, San Francisco, and Toronto. His most recent accolades include, in 1992, an appointment as "Officier" of the order of arts and literature of the French Republic, an honorary degree in 1993 from the Rhode Island School of Design, and in 1994 the IF Award Design Kopfe from Industrie Forum Design in Hannover; in 1996 he was awarded both an honorary doctoral degree at the Royal College of Art of London and a design prize by the Brooklyn Museum in New York.

Marco Zanini

Born in Trent, Italy, in 1954, Marco Zanini graduated from architecture school in Florence in 1976. In 1980 he cofounded Sottsass Associates and is now managing director of the firm. He was also one of the founders of the Memphis group, for which he designed the various collections that were later exhibited in important museums and galleries around the world and presented in leading design magazines. For Sottsass Associates he has designed some of the firm's most important projects, covering the full range of design areas in which the firm works.

Johanna Grawunder

Johanna Grawunder was born in San Diego, California, in 1961. In 1984 she received her degree in architecture from the California State Polytechnic University in San Luis Obispo and Florence, Italy. In 1985 she moved to Milan, where she joined Sottsass Associates, becoming a partner in the firm in 1989. Since then she has designed some of the firm's most important architecture projects, including Wolf House in Colorado, Olabuenaga House in Hawaii, Yuko House in Tokyo, the Contemporary Furniture Museum in Ravenna, Italy, the Golf Club and Resort in China, a residential village, also in China, and other houses in Australia, Singapore, and Belgium.

Mike Ryan

Born in Long Beach, California, in 1961, Mike Ryan received an architecture degree from California State Polytechnic University in San Luis Obispo and Florence (1985). In 1985 he exhibited his own work in the Third International Architecture Exhibition at the Venice Biennale, the same time at which he moved to Milan and joined Sottsass Associates. A partner since 1989, he has produced a number of interior design and architecture projects, most notably the interiors for the new Milan Malpensa 2000 airport and the Flower Dome baseball stadium in Osaka, Japan, the Zibibbo bar in Fukuoka, Japan, Cei House in Tuscany, Italy, the Alitalia VIP lounge system, and an urban development project for the city of Inchon, Korea.

James Irvine

James Irvine was born in London in 1958. In 1984 he graduated from the Royal College of Art. He moved to Italy in the same year and joined the Olivetti Design Studio. In 1987 he relocated to Tokyo to carry out industrial design research for Toshiba. He has been a partner in Sottsass Associates since 1993; he is currently in charge of the firm's design department, where he has created highly praised designs for clients such as Siemens, Kaldewei, Zumtobel, Telecom, Zanotta, and Ideal Standard.

Mario Milizia

Mario Milizia was born in Milan in 1965. In 1986 he obtained a diploma in graphic design. He joined Sottsass Associates in 1989, becoming a partner in the firm in 1993. As head of the firm's graphic design department, he has produced important graphic design and coordinated-image projects for the Venice Biennale, the Centre Georges Pompidou in Paris, Olivetti, Siemens, Alessi, Abet Laminati, Erg Petroli, and Rizzoli. In 1998 he founded the magazine FA. His designs and installations are exhibited in museums and galleries in Italy and elsewhere, including the Mamco in Geneva, Switzerland, the Magasin in Grenoble, France, and the De Appel in Amsterdam, The Netherlands.

Christopher Redfern

Born in Burton-Upon-Trent, England, in 1972, Christopher Redfern received a degree in design after studying in England and Germany. In 1994 he started to work as an industrial designer in Hong Kong and China. He later moved to Stockholm, where he worked in an architecture firm. In 1996 he joined Sottsass Associates and in 1999 became a partner. He currently heads the design department. With Sottsass Associates he has produced designs for Seiko, Telecom Italia, Kaldewei, Agfa, and Siemens.

Bibliography

General Bibliography

Ambaz, E. Italy: The New Domestic Landscape, Museum of Modern Art, New York, 1972.

Branzi, A. Il design italiano: 1964/1990, Electa, Milan, 1996.

————. La casa calda, Idea Book, Milan, 1984.

————. Moderno, posterno, millenario, Studio Forma, Milan, 1980.

Burney, J. Ettore Sottsass, Trefoil, London, 1991.

De Bure, G. Ettore Sottsass, Jr, Rivages, Paris, 1987.

De Castro, F. Ettore Sottsass: scrap-book, Milan, 1976.

Der Fall Memphis oder die Neomoderne, Hochschule Für Gestaltung, Offenbach, 1984.

Design als Postulat. Am Beispiel Italien, IDZ, Berlin, 1973.

Ettore Sottsass, Centre Georges Pompidou, Paris, 1994.

Ettore Sottsass: de l'object fini à la fin de l'object, Musée des Arts Décoratifs, Paris, 1976.

Ettore Sottsass: Drawings over Four Decades, Ikon Gallery, Frankfurt, 1990.

Ettore Sottsass sr. architetto, Electa, Milan, 1991.

Ferrari, F. Ettore Sottsass: tutta la ceramica, Allemandi, Turin, 1996.

Fossati, P. Il design in Italia: 1945–72, Einaudi, Turin, 1972.

Gaon, I. Ettore Sottsass, Jr., Israel Museum, Jerusalem, 1978.

Hoger, H. Ettore Sottsass, Jr., Wasmuth, Berlin, 1993.

Horn, R. Memphis: Object, Furniture, and Pattern, Running Press, Philadelphia, 1985.

Kontinuität von Leben und Werk: Arbeiten 1955–1975 von Ettore Sottsass, Berlin, 1976.

Martorana, A. Ettore Sottsass: storie e progetti di un designer italiano, Alinea, Florence, 1983.

Memphis: ceramiques, argent, verre 1981–1987, Musée d'Art Décoratifs, Marseille, 1991.

Navone, P., and B. Orlandoni, Architettura radicale, Milan, 1974.

Pettena, G. La città invisibile: architettura sperimentale 1965/75, Florence, 1983.

Radice, B. Ettore Sottsass, Electa, Milan, 1993.

————. Gioielli di architetti, Electa, Milan, 1987.

————. Memphis: ricerche, esperienze, risultati, fallimenti e successi del nuovo design, Electa, Milan, 1984.

————. Memphis: The New International Style, Electa, Milan, 1981.

Sambonet, G. Ettore Sottsass, Mobili e qualche arredamento, Mondadori, Milan, 1985.

Santini, P.C., Facendo mobili con . . . , Florence, 1977.

Sato, K. Alchymia. Neverending Italian Design, Tokyo, 1985.

Shapira, N. Design Process Olivetti: 1908–1978, Wright Art Gallery, Los Angeles, 1979.

Sottsass Associati, Rizzoli, New York, 1988.

Sottsass Associati, Architetture 1985/1990, Milan, 1990.

Sottsass Associati, Arrêt sur l'image, Edizioni l'Archivolto, Milan, 1993.

Sottsass Associati, Design 1985/1990, Milan, 1990.

Sottsass Associati, Dodici interni, Terrazzo, Milan, 1996.

Sottsass Associati, Graphic Design 1985/1990, Milan, 1990.

Sparke, P. Ettore Sottsass, Jr., Design Council, London, 1982.

Thomé, P. Ettore Sottsass, Jr.: De l'object à l'environment, Geneva, 1991.

By Ettore Sottsass

Glass Works, Vitrum, Venice, 1998.

Lo specchio di Saffo, Postdesign, Milan, 1998.

Architetture indiane e dintorni, Naples, 1998.

151 Drawings, Gallery Ma, Tokyo, 1997.

The Curious Mr Sottsass: Photo Design and Desire, Thames & Hudson, London, 1996.

Memorie de Chine, Gallery Mourmans, Knokke, 1996.

Big & Small Works, Gallery Mourmans, Knokke, 1995.

Walls, Terrazzo, ed., Milan, 1995.

Ceramics, Stemmle, Zurich, 1995.

Adesso però—Reiseerinnerungen, Hatje Verlag, Hamburg, 1994.

La darrera oportunitat d'esser avantguarda, Centre d'Art Santa Monica, Barcelona, 1993.

Rovine, Design Gallery, Milan, 1992.

Advanced Studies 1986–1990, Yamagiwa Art Fundation, Tokyo, 1990.

Design Metaphors, Idea Books, Milan, 1988.

Bharata, Design Gallery, Milan, 1988.

C'est pas facile la vie, Il Melangolo, Milan, 1987.

Curio cabinet, mirror, chairs, tables, sideboards, pedestal, credenzas, Blum Helman Gallery, New York, 1987.

Esercizio Formale no. 2, Studio Forma/Alchimia, Milan, 1980.

Esercizio Formale, Milan, 1979.

Miljo for en ny planet, National Museum, Stockholm, 1969.

Photography Credits